Minstrel Boy

Dagric Alan

Edward Gaskell
DEVON

First published 2009
Edward Gaskell publishers
Old Sawmill
Grange Road
Bideford
Devon EX39 4AS

isbn (10) 1 -906769 -14 -1
isbn (13) 978 -1 -906769 -14 -7

© Dagric Alan
web: www.dagricalan.com
email: dagricalan@aol.com
illustrations & cover Sue Podbery

Minstrel Boy

Dagric Alan

All rights reserved. No part of this publication may be reproduced, stored in a retrieval system, or transmitted in any form by any means electronic, mechanical, photocopying, scanning, recording or otherwise, without the prior written permission of the publishers.

Typeset, printed and bound by
Lazarus Press
Caddsdown Business Park
Bideford
Devon
EX39 3DX
www.lazaruspress.com

Lazarus Press

Dagric Alan

The author's childhood was spent initially in the South West London suburb of Streatham before a move to Wallington, Surrey where the end of the road led to rurality in the form of small holdings leading to Chipstead Valley and Banstead Downs. With the ability to roam freely his love of the countryside developed.

School lessons had earlier been interrupted by air raids which became a way of life and like so many of his generation Dagric can claim to have been 'under fire' more than many a member of the armed forces, having been bombed, land-mined, incarcerated by incendiaries and, with a friend, machine gunned by an enemy plane.

Showing little aptitude nor interest in the school curriculum beyond English Literature and History he was encouraged to write by his form master who on occasions put his acerbic wit to one side to treat kindly what he considered an emerging talent.

A visit one evening to his, by now, ex-master confirmed for Dagric that as a twenty year old he had made the crossing from boyhood to manhood when his mentor said 'I usually have a brandy and soda around this time, will you join me?'

Editing two local magazines at seventeen and having pieces accepted by the *New Statesman* in John Freeman's time, as well as articles for other periodicals, writing had to be put aside in order to devote time to studying and it took a bereavement to bring him back to writing, not in prose nor in poetry but in the unique style he has made his own.

When National Service called he joined the Royal Air Force where he spent most of the time at Bentley Priory, R.A.F. Fighter Command Headquarters. Here his horizons were widened by the eclectic mix of officer veterans now consigned to flying desks, career sergeants and the sportsmen, athletes, writers and actors, plumbers and pianists that National Service had thrown together. Towards the end of his service Dagric was instrumental in the detection, arraignment and conviction of a Russian spy whose trial he feared would result in the putting back of his demobilisation date.

Returning to civilian life he endured a stint in marine insurance in the City of London before entering the shipping industry and qualifying as a Chartered Shipbroker. Eventually fed up with playing commercial politics he gave up city life to form his own insurance and finance brokerage where he was able to give free rein to his preference to support the right of the individual and champion many lost causes.

For all those who believed.

My very special thanks are due to Andrew and Valerie Eastman
who made it happen

to Sue Podbery for her wonderful illustrations

and to my publisher,
Edward Gaskell
for his ideas, encouragement,
and sense of fun

and, of course,
to the girl with the autumn sun in her hair.

CONTENTS

Minstrel Boy

1	A SUSSEX CHRISTMAS GREETING	14
2	KAY	15
3	HANNAH	16
4	PAM	17
5	TETTY TITANIUM	18
6	CONTESSA MARIE	19
7	STEYNING JOHN	20
8	BIG TONY	22
9	MARTIN	24
10	LEARNING LATIN	26
11	HARD HATS	28
12	IMPRESSIONS	30
13	FATHER GROGAN'S BICYCLE	32
14	CREATION	33
15	RESURRECTION	35
16	A MYSTERY	37
17	DIXIE	39
18	LISTENING	41
19	CALCETO DAYS	43
20	MY, MY ATHENIAN PIE	45
21	RED BRICK	46
22	ANGELUS BELL	48

CONTENTS

Around the Camp Fire

23	GAUJO BOY	51
24	ECUMENICAL WITH THE TRUTH	55
25	HOUSE CLEARANCE	56
26	JAM AND JERUSALEM	58
27	JOHN	60
28	COUSIN PETER	61
29	TALK OF THE DEVIL	62
30	ACHTUNG SPITFIRE	65
31	L'ALGERIE FRANCAISE	67
32	DOWN AT JOHNNY IDLE'S	69
33	HOME COUNTIES SARAH	71
34	HOLIDAYS	73
35	NIGHT VISION	74
36	TOAD IN BLUE JEANS	77
37	WOLLEN HAT	79
38	SOMETHING IN THE CITY	81
39	SING DUSTY SING	83
40	O'GRADY	84
41	SMALL BUSINESS	85
42	RETURN TICKET	86
43	UP ON A VISIT	88
44	WINDOWS	91
45	POST	92
46	SAN JABANGO DAYS	93
47	TIME	96
48	ICARUS ABOVE STEYNING BOWL	97
49	THE POETS WORE GREY SUITS	98
50	JOBS AND JAM	100
51	A CHANCE ENCOUNTER	101
52	TWO LOVES	103

CONTENTS

Over the Hills and Far Away

53	A VITAL PIECE OF EVIDENCE	106
54	HOME JAMES	110
55	THE OTHER HALF	111
56	THE DIVVIE	113
57	TRAVELLING	115
58	THE NEWS TODAY	116
59	THE CHURCHES GREAT FOUNDATIONS	117
60	LAMPING	120
61	IS THERE ANYBODY LEFT IN ALBANIA?	121
62	OLD KING COLE	122
63	DINNER FOR FIVE	124
64	SHADES OF GILDAS	126
65	ON THE TRAIN	127
66	A MAN OF THE TOWN	129
67	COUNTRY LIVING	131
68	MOTHER'S DAY	132
69	SUMMER	133
70	CRISPIN SHEEPE	136
71	ANNIE PHOTOGRAPH	139
72	TIME II	141
73	THREE BLIND MICE	142
74	IRISH DANCING	144
75	TIME III	147
76	WISE MONKEY	149
77	MY HOUSE	150
78	THE MAN FROM HEATHFIELD	152
79	IN THE CLUB	155
80	QUONDAM TRAVEL	156
81	TUBBY TAYLOR	157
82	SUSSEX PAEN	159
83	ST VALENTINE'S DAY	161
84	OLD ERNIE	162
85	TELL ME ABOUT JO'BURG	165
86	THE RELICT	167
87	BREAKING BREAD	169
88	A BAWD'S EYE VIEW	171
89	DEVONSHIRE DUMPLING	173
90	KNOCK, KNOCK - WHO'S THERE?	174
91	CHARLIE	176
92	FOLLOW THE STAR	177
93	FINE FARE	180

Minstrel Boy

A SUSSEX CHRISTMAS GREETING

From Chichester the choir sings true
 A message that is both old and new
Of Shepherds and Kings and a Child's birth.
 At the Cross people mingle and greet
One another, and depart for turkey feast
 And plum pudding sweet.

From Middleton a soft warm greeting
 Borne on feathery tamarisk meeting
 winding, puddled, rutted lanes and
 oak-lined fields with Hereford cattle
In St. Nicholas Church lies Babe in Crib
 With toys and rattle.

From sleepy Arundel a God's Day Wish;
 A late start - but not yet prepare the dish.
First coffee, toast and leisurely promenade
 Past the Castle, down the hill to the Black Rabbit
Surely we did this last year - getting a habit?

 From Bury Hill
 Where scattered ashes lay not still,
But live again in regenerated earth,
 And the Spirit breathes over the loved Arun view.
 From Bury Hill, God's blessing, too

KAY

Corn coloured hair, china blue eyes.
The winds of Connamara honed your beauty.
Priest-ridden, you crossed the water
And nursed the terminally sick.
With your high intelligence and rare sense of humour
You could, I think
Have risen to the height of your profession.
But my dear - you loved a drink!

HANNAH
(The Amateur Whore)

    You traded on the Taurus connection
Our birthdays were closer than that
Were you really a blue eyed Jewess
Or a quick witted scouse?

    Endlessly circulating in pubs and bars
You exchanged laughs and kisses
for drinks and meals and accommodation
'Hannah! Over here Hannah', you answered the call.
And dreamed of singing in the Albert Hall.
    In the Camelot Club you entertained the city slickers
But fell off your stool
- for once you were wearing knickers.
At evening's close sometimes strangely not tight
On leaving, shrewdly you became a Poet of the Soul
And occasionally a Queen of the Night.

PAM

   Surrounded by your antiques and gifties,
with close cropped hair above tight trousers and sweater.
Side on, face obscured you could have been taken for a feller.
   Then the laughter in your eyes, the brass, the cheek.
   Confirmed the psyche.

'Put your hands down on the counter.
   - you need a ring for your pinkie.
When we're finished here - how about a little drinkie?'
Woodbines and gin and tonics in the Kosher Horses
You stood out like a character from Lovejoy.
   And - you-did-love-joy.

TETTY TITANIUM

They say you were even more beautiful then
One brief moment on a Roman road nearly robbed you of
                                                                               your life
Almost the world had space in the hub
of the wheel of influence.
Italianate surgery rebuilt the cranium
and fashioned you anew with a deal of titanium.

The mind and the soul intact as before
Travelling from East to East
In Bow to build your own cultural salon
spurning the suits, artistically eloquent of tongue and eye,
toiling tirelessly - such unconfined joy,
When at last you made Ralph a good Jewish boy.

I'm sorry I missed the Whitechapel exhibition
One Friday I'll come and sup with tradition
And jointly we'll consign 'them' to perdition.
Till then Tetty dear know this as the truth -
    The best of the rest could never compare
with the lovely Israeli with the so-classy air.

CONTESSA MARIE

Standing on one foot close hemmed to suffocation
streetwise, handbag firmly underarm and possessions
                                      in plastic carrier
you endure an underground eternity to Victoria Station.
Free at last to board a Southern Coastal train
and carefully evaluate the seating alternatives.
Spurning space next to the lady wreathed in trumpets of
                                      Givenchy
selecting instead the buffet car.
Continuing with *The Times* crossword - nothing raunchy
just time enough to sip a vodka and light up.

Released at the first stop, enigmatic you cross
halogen lit concrete Croydon.
Sometimes the nun, sometimes in the carefully crafted eyes
other virtues race
La Belle Dame sans Merci?
Who penetrates the Giaconda face.

STEYNING JOHN

Money's for spending, life's for living
and then you're gone
said Steyning John

    The keen eye that can work in squash
or pick the ball from the penthouse in tennis
can also detect a Stubbs from 'of the school of'
at twenty paces
    Preferring the functional beauty of oak
to the flounciness of walnut or mahogany
The simple marine oil to the overdressed whoreishness
of jewish renaissance
He is a man of high principles
concealing feelings comes easier to him
than to most Englishmen
Gregarious yet making few friends.
Enjoying the physicality of fitness
and the open air.
Trekking in Patagonia, outdoing Kerouac
and riding the great Trans-Siberian
a Lonesome Traveller.

Bereft of the Players Navy cut beard
He will still answer the call and crew a yacht
back from Greece
for beer money and miles on the log.
    When skippering his own vessel and running 'gainst
                                                   the tide
he takes no prisoners.
You work until you drop

In La Vendee it was 'no surrender'
and here it is 'no compromise'.
This same stubbornness prohibits him working for
or with fools
And makes him ride the South Downs
all day in 'middle cog'
Yet seeing the late afternoon sun
slip behind Chanctonbury Ring
suddenly pedalling like a demon defying logic
in the attempt to ride into that warm circle
 of light that ever moves further away.

 A romantic? Surely not.
When work or sport are done a pint of Ruddles
is a salve to be taken in a local hostelry.
Strolling past the cricket green
he lifts his eyes unto the hills
on his way home.

In this ancient now portless town
He has his berth.
Steyning has his hearth
And Steyning has his heart
And one day surely will have his bones.
But in the meantime lazily,
softly, the wind moans.
        The song of Steyning John
           'Life is the game
                And more of the same!'

BIG TONY

He wanders up and down the town
a bit like Wee Willie Winkie in his nightgown.
Except the garb is generally sweater
and loose wide-legged trousers that unsuccessfully
seek to conceal the ample girth.
Like a liner he has his regular port of call.
The antique emporium, the side street grocers and
the pavement lined with special offers.
New menus for the Shalimar Nights,
the monthly list for the bookshop
catalogues for the World of Pine.
At Mr Bryson - Fishmonger of repute -
he surprisingly buys Caribbean Pink
and talks of making delicate lemon sauce.

A sociable man with a somewhat Pickwickian air,
in checks it would be Wooster or Frank Richards.
A conversationalist whose wit is somewhat acerbic
an entertainer - it was ever thus -
knowing they laugh at him.
A lone printer
not for him the joshing petty men
who played silly tricks and talked of
unions and Fathers of Chapel
and employment
walking and working alone
when very busy he will get Tom-sixpenny-Guiness
from The Eagle to lend a hand - but that's different.

Arriving back at his home berth
turning the key in the door of
the two up two down period terraced house,
he calls his 'drum'
he thinks of her.
Did she cook and clean the oven?
He cannot remember, but does recall
she cleared out the account with the Abbey National.
The departed, wife for all too short a while
who up and left him with a note
when all he needed was a smile
indicating someone cared
for this overweight ponderous gentleman.
But no she did not care
and in the stealthy silence of the house
bearing the many cicatrix of hurt
he thinks once more of
work, regular little voyages, visits to the pub and
    being thought - A Character.

MARTIN

'I've no education' he said.
Replying to the 'what do you do?' question.
There was always so much stuff going on at school
Too busy to learn - they claimed he played the fool
and refused to listen to the masters clitter clatter
'There's always work for a well set up young feller'
-      so it really didn't matter.
Running with the gang he dreamed lesson times away
and preferred the Liffey and the streets around
to the un-navigable rivers of formal education.
Leaving the lesson house behind as soon as he was able.

Working at 'McGuires Construction' for a spell
then body hardened he graduated to London
for better pay but a meaner way of life.
The work was plentiful and as one job finished
There was always another for
a well set up young feller.
When the depression came and the laying off began
the brickies and the chippies and the plumbers
did odd jobs and survived
For those like him - the ordinary man
the cold and the damp took up
permanent lodging in the bones.
The D.S.S. clerks showed contempt for the queue
and shut their ears to its moans.

The jet black hair started to turn at twenty five
and was now iron grey set.
From time to time they offered retraining courses
Government plans to re-deploy human resources;
but anything to do with reading, figures or computers
would always be beyond him.
With no education he did not belong.
Neither did he on the last visit to Dublin.
A quickly changing city and with no job to boast of
a no longer well set up feller could not belong.
He still dreamed, watched, listened and
remembered the old stories
- and became a judge of people.

    Life had become a matter of drawing the Giro
Roll your own and three pints at lunch time.
That's how he came to be in the Bull sitting at the table
with the three of them, listening to their business talk,
exchanging the odd comment with the big one about
the cricket on the box.
Watching the open mouthed enjoyment and
perceiving behind
the beard and public school tones the infant of yesteryear
He'd asked what they did
and the girl returned the question like a ball in play
with her precise words and earnest way.
He learned what they did
and felt warm when they left
Knowing the man he thought was a barrister
the one he liked best
Was a teller of tales, a minstrel, come out of the west.

LEARNING LATIN

Like a bird we swooped up and down
                                  the hills
That lit by rows of headlamps
seemed to torch processional ways
Traversing the Chiltern Hundreds
Then by tented Henley on the Thames where bereft of breeze
in the still air your perfume lingered
as though the town unable to
make you stay wanted a remembrance.

At Marlow's Complete Angler you spoke
of driving tests and hand signals
(you use them still - all the time)
and showed continental flair
on until
Stealing a parking space from a clumsy jag
We climbed the stair, under the vine clad arch
to the trattoria
High speed Italian gained us access to a table
animation and service.
In candles glow your candescence
warmed the room
the scarf at your throat pointed to your elegance.
I ate one handed a prisoner of your affection.

Later short skirt hitched
to let a shapely leg straddle the bed
tactile as ever you said what was in your head.
Did I understand you? Every accented word?
I listened! And I heard.
But let Catullus speak -

                        Resurgam.

HARD HATS

    They're doing up the barn in Ancton Lance
Putting it back to use again
The roof is bare the slates have gone
new struts and old provide a vaulted backbone
that covered will keep the inhabitants snug o'night
    But that's a long way off

A hard hat area
wire fence and padlock keep bare walls
and a dripping tap from inquisitive visitors.
The stable block and tall open fodder store
with high metal roof remain on the side
defiant of plans to be gentrified.
　　The barn interior is stripped bare
waiting plastering, flooring, plumbing,
walls to separate kitchen and living rooms,
bedrooms - will they get a gallery up there?

　　All in the hands of the architect man
who visits intermittently when he can.
No more home for beasts and crops
we're down to one farm where there used to be three.
The architect says 'it's all down to me.
The planners agreed, my clients are keen
what Laura Ashley can do just has to be seen'.
Will the stables resound with pony club squeals
and the forecourt be home for 'black man's wheels?'
The architect says its all down to me
- my clients needed no coercion
their ambition's to live - in a barn conversion.

IMPRESSIONS

    Fairy lights in the windows
A warmth of fruity hair-sprays behind which lurks
a faint ammoniacal smell
reminiscent of an eastern whore's perfume
concealing advancing decay.
    Coloured roots and silver streaks
the quite hish of nylon crossing legs.
At number five the auburn hue
taps her nails - so much to do.

    Mistletoe above every basin
chairs in a row, each with its acolyte.
Stylists who dance attendance, complete the
complicated ritual and exchange the finished product
for a new customer.
Affectionate greetings inconsequential chatter
and some revelations made in this one to one confessional
of things that really matter.
    Beth and Liz, Shaz and Jayne
sharing secrets again and again
And George who struts his stuff
at last deciding it's good enough -
For Mrs Henson 'Deirdre' she murmurs as he presses her
                                                      palm

Eyes locked in congress they say their goodbyes
'On Thursday we fly to Geneva', she sighs.
'But after Christmas I'll be back
- can you fit me in before the New Year
- bring me up to scratch - I rely on you dear.'
A pressi for Beth and coins in the staff box.
A deep smile at George as she tosses her locks
and coat open sweeps through the door and departs.
    Swinging by the butchers with its row of
turkeys, stripped of feathers, legs straight out bound together
in supplemental pose.
    They too prepared for Christmas.

    Jayne gazes past the window
sees the Mercedes door close.
Another half-hour and it's home for tea.
'One day, like George I'll own my own salon
    'Impressions it'll be - just for me'.

FATHER GROGAN'S BICYCLE

Female and elderly, inherited from his aunt
it must now be among the elders of the parish
A pre-war Rudge Whitworth
still giving sterling service
and worth to its owner it's considerable weight in gold.
Familiar with all the local highways and byways
short cuts and ginnels
out in all weathers from summer's heat to winter's cold.

From the presbytery to the church is down hill
-      the slight front wheel wobble less noticeable on the way back.
Squeaking its way to and from the Women's Institute
the Wednesday Club, Choir practice and Bible study
and on Saturdays to be on the touch line
giving support to the football team in conditions wet and muddy
It clocks up the miles.

Visiting the sick and conveying its
fit but rotund owner to confessions
it is on nodding terms with all
-      yet keeps its counsel
of the stealthy visits to
the black and unrepentant sheep who share their
whiskey and humour with the kindly shepherd
appreciating his concern for their physical and spiritual needs
and in this concealment
allowing them not to lose face.

Pressed in God's service it waits long
for the Blessed Trinity
a clean and
a liberal dose of Three-In-One oil.

'CREATION'

 The command request carries from one room to the next
'Help you with the shopping, go to the cleaners,
wash the kitchen floor - I must call in at Tesco's,
cut the front lawn, put petrol in the car -
oh is that where you are!
Mother is coming on Saturday, the house must look nice.'
Another voice, more questions, more chatter.
Don't tell me - she's bright.
'She will be a comfort and give much needed
support which I am too wrapped up in myself to provide.
Discipline is what is needed, sort out my day.
Fit my writing in between, or after the other tasks.
You have to cope with a million and one things
all the time, it needs planning not moping.'

 I'm not moping, mourning. Mourning for the mystical
dawn chorus, the inspirational fresh day-break
dew on the grass, gossamer webs in the hedgerows.
The new morning smells now buried.
Buried in the whirring droning washing machine
intent on completing a cycle
by putting clean clothes on ever active children.

Voices several octaves higher than my brain's acceptance level.
Faces that insist on being within sight
mouths that flap incessantly - the continual chatter
tells you - you tell me - they are bright.

   What we have replicated with the fruitful seed
now forms a noisy demanding barrier to the quite reflection I need.
There is no art without misery the man said.
Such saws - ancient platitudes - now pall.
I only know

        The Death Knell for Art is -
        The Pram in the Hall

'Resurrection' was written in memory of a long time friend and truth to tell it pretty well wrote itself. So, with poetic license in respect of the Emmaus Road. . . . . . for Lawrence

RESURRECTION

April warmth on my neck.
New mown grass, daffodil and
hyacinth smell around me
The fork prized open the earth
revealing a tracery
of delicate fibrous roots and
multi-legged scaly life
from this fresh turned peck.
On straightening I saw
through the elder branches
The blond hair, open smile
and wide shoulders.

I am the resurrection and life

How long is it my fellow strategist
since we last met?
Even then setting out the board that only we
could read.
Perceiving that but one of us would
see harvest time from sown seed.
The still active answer-phone voice
Full of measured gravitas
Is not needed as a reminder
For the head carries all friendship's recordings.

Who so believieth in Me shall not Perish

Why look among the dead

The boisterous laugh travelled well
over the years and places
infecting many with a sense of fun
and camaraderie.
Maturer than your brother's daredevil
spit-on-the-world grin
Kindly authoritarian at work and play
You put them through their paces.

He is alive

When day slipped into night and
The bright moon in the indigo star-less sky
lit the way past the four-barred gate
into the lane and the trees cut clawed shadows
on the field.
We walked in companionable silence
following the dog
Three on a road - and it was after all, Easter.

In South London 'Jack-the-Lad' language a strange woman is
'a mystery' - in horsey circles Regency slang lingers on and a horse
is a 'prad'. A Romany is sometimes called an Egyptian.

A MYSTERY

   Sitting in the corner of The Eagle
nursing a half when John-the-clock walks in with a mystery.
He's sprauncy-like, showing his Singapore rolex
calling the landlord 'Les'
she's tall - dark not fair - not Pam - but that's history.

   Brown arm on the table, large VATs
John fusses his chair, he's out to please.
Ada slides from her stool
scooping up her hearthrug, calls 'Cheerio dears, that's that.'
Making for her retirement flat.
a life of gin and limes and good-boys.

   Big Tony obscures my view and blots out my ears
'No sooner printed than it's changed
work my rollocks off all morning
all this fairying about, 1500 down the drain
I'll charge him for it but that's not the point
I should be - Jesus what's that noise!'
The landlord savvies and kills the music
new glasses and bottles - another round
squinting round Tone, I glimpse
the unchecked change trousered.
He's up for it.

   Fishy Fred arrives with a pasty
buys a round and the Tone drones on.

Heads together nodding, laughing,
leaning back in amazement, then forward again
serious chatter I can't hear
with these noisy prats on either side
talking themselves up over their beer.
John's hands on the table propel him half-up
anticipating the answer - 'more of the same?'
He's like a young pup.
Is she up for it?

White teeth tear open a packet of nuts
un-ringed hands traverse from bag to mouth.
John writes in his notebook - has he got her number?
She scrumples the packet and crosses her legs.
The others oblivious, is it only me I wonder?

Fred tries another tack 'How's your auntie Vi?'
Tone won't be moved.
'Back in her drum, I'll get to her bye and bye.'
No music yet
so the governor's on the q'vie
He clears the table, John orders again.
Fred says 'It's your round' - that's a good try.
Faint click from the back where the lads play pool.
Tone gets them in.

   'Time's money' says Fred
'I must carry me hence.'
Tony looks round and waddles to the gents.
With no sign of damage she gets to her feet
passing my table they move to the door
lifting his wrist so the hands are plain
she says 'Thanks for the treat.
time to feed my prad.'

     Blimey, he's landed an Egyptian!

DIXIE

I saw you again yesterday
crossing the car-park
there was no mistaking that walk, the little hippy lilt.
Clinging lemon dress matching the hair
slight hesitation - head a-tilt
a gambler still.

An odds-calculating gambler
winning at pool, name that tune,
beggar your neighbour, find the lady,
first past the post - they'll be here soon
bridge and darts, a game of Mickey Mouse
all grist to a sparky feisty scouse.

The assurance at the interview,
gambling on learning the job from someone else
for them to take you at face value
- always good - and not call the bluff.
Swerving, pace changing side stepping slickly swiftly
ever seeking a way through the maze of life
as a libation to the gods you would offer
- if you lost the wager - as a lark -
to stand bare arsed in the car-park
    and whistle Dixie.

    I saw you again yesterday
crossing the park.
And the years could not condemn.
Observing a slight hesitation
I waited for the defiant gesture
knowing, you never could whistle worth a damn

LISTENING

Crossing the carpet clad entrance
Hearing a murmur from behind the reception desk
I listen
to louder voices and a no-guests-to-consider
raucous laugh.
Entering the coffee lounge
I listen.
Detecting at last movement and saucer stacking
way back in the sacrosanct service area.
Coins on the counter bring forth the waiter.
He listens
As I order and annex the window settee
with large table.
My sipping behind *The Independent*
is interrupted and I am forced
to listen.

Settling round the next table
that marks the dimly lit corridor like bowels of the lounge
The women bray with volume
wearing like armour
all the assurance of middle class empty-headed up-bringing.
Clad in twin sets and the best of Berketex and Evans
Hand and knee patting septuagenarians
their only topic holidays
Going to - back from
seeing and learning nothing.
Contributing after every account mechanical laughter.
Eliciting dutiful lagging-behind haw-haws from their men.

These were in their day
something in the city
or successful in running the inherited business into the
ground.

With all the insouciance of minor public school upbringing
They never listened.
For it wasn't what you knew but whom
A maxim that has served them well
and will do, to the tomb

Two sports jackets face the ladies
checked shirts and crested ties - the empty chair
has gone to another table its previous occupant where?
The third member of the trio dated blazer
and flared flannels is no more.
He saw the quack and the consultant Johnny
who talked to them both
but she did not listen
and now he's left her blames him and says
'he would not listen'.
The waiter's enquiry if more hot milk is needed
like the squeezing by young couple's 'excuse me's'
go unheeded.
They spend their lives
not listening.

Outside in the street watching
the crowd by the registry office
throwing confetti and shouting greetings
Dodging the Saturday shoppers' meetings
and traffic pausing for the
Sally Army band
I listen
Knowing the coffee set have made this busy street
a relative oasis of calm.
Knowing that next Saturday, arriving early
I will again deny them their window table.

CALCETO DAYS

Calceto Farm lies off the road along a narrow track.
Past the farmhouse around the bend
the massive stone granary stands sentinel like, all superior,
marking the end of vehicle access.
Perfectly formed two inch gossamer spiders' webs
adorn the discarded iron gate
sharing against the wall space with Dave's workhorse estate.
Yielding easily to my shoulder charge the no longer sticking
door drops me vigorously into the cool interior.
'Just dropped in, me old biscuit?' enquires Dave, the sometime
bookseller who has risen from
basement floor to lofty workshop
and resumed again his original craft of cabinet maker.

Dwarfed by the tall vaulted ceiling
his work appears scattered like an exhibition in a cathedral.
A work bench here, pine work-tops waiting the insertion of a
sink leaning against a dresser there.
In the centre almost spanning the room tall book shelves and
cupboards under, in three sections commissioned by a private
library in Wiltshire - 'One of my old connections.'
As a backdrop to the craftsman's art sit piles of wood
the raw fuel for future tasks.
Heart and bone warming May
masks the memory of the deep winter chill with the only heat
a small stove in the drying room. From the eight by ten window, once the loading bay we can see right over the flatlands
almost to the sea's edge
where Dutch vessels dredge and build sea defences.

Where couples oil each other on towels
dogs chase balls and boys chase girls
and small children cast themselves on surfboards hoping to
ride the waves right up and onto
the golden compacted sand.
Where mothers sun themselves and see
but do not comprehend the returning undertow.
On the eye-line stands the cosmetic factory its ugliness
a tribute to the planning committee who would, not say no

Seated on an upturned box before the freshly made
too hot to handle tea mugs that will leave wet rings on the
bench we relax in conversation.
Hemmingway, Chandler and Dylon Thomas.
Global warming, exhaust emission and pollution
('Shoot the buggers - that's the solution!')
John Moore, Betjeman and Laurie Lee.
Sip by sip we finish the tea.
At last
reaching in the pocket of the long white overall
for his tin Dave rolls a last cigarette.
'The light's gone now, reckon I've earned me pay,
it's time we called it a day'.
Rising we end
another Calceto Day

MY, MY ATHENIAN PIE

George came today, emerging from the Volvo
Laughing, happy, blue denim trews jumbo white tee
and scarlet sweater tied by the arms round the middle.
Opening the back to reveal trays and boxes
pitta humous octopi and olives
cucumber and mint, wine and taramasalata.
yes I could find a tomato.

Sitting in the garden, sun warming our arms
he talked of the film industry, LA had lost its charms.
Music? Lamenting the decline of the ballad
drizzling olive oil on the salad
art, literature, cities choked in diesel fumes
deviation and improvisation like a jazz composition
free ranging conversation that at last returned
to the point of entry.
Business advice sought and given.
A commitment to the future.
With words of far-off lands
the afternoon slipped by and at last he left with an
invitation to Athens - but England was the place to settle!

Later I walked through the lane to the beach
over the tide-washed sands.
A perfume of cattle tamarisk and sea
meeting the nostrils and salt on the lips
Light headed on air and wine
scrambling, breathing deeply, remembering the tips -
   Beware of Greeks bearing dips.

RED BRICK

I know a place where the red brick grows
where the keen cold blast of commerce blows
a place where the farmer no longer hoes
where the tractors gone and the digger toils.
The battle's lost - to the builder the spoils,
And the red brick grows.

Familiarity runs through the never ending rows of
retirement bungalows -
where the surviving partner wears the armchair and loneliness heavily.
Where the relentless tick of the Faustus clock
that sits in the hall
can be heard in the still early hours
from the warm cocoon of the bed -
red brick sitting either side of the ever busier
fuel choked coastal road
that prevents the inhabitants enjoying
the green view and the sea view they thought they'd bought.
And we speed by to the country.

To the velvet cushioned chalk and flint of the downs
to the harebells, butterflies and grazing sheep.
To the narrow winding lanes flanked by browsing Herefords
and fresh tilled acres blanketed in birds
that lead to villages, pubs and familiar shops
where they call us by our names.
The planned 'to leave-us-in-peace' by-pass
led to the out of town supermarket
that in turn sliced trade from the villages
and the empty sites became charity shops.

Charity is not in the poke-it-in-infill application.
Agricultural land it seems is a land fit for a builder's nation
and open to bids.
Men in high places
tell us, in a relentless spin of
lies that conceal truths and truths that conceal lies -
that we must
make room for more housing,
-   and plan to theme our countryside,
with golf courses, farm museums, visitor centres
and olde worlde tea shoppes,
that will satisfy these town bred leaf peepers
that they are conserving the country whilst stuffing it full of
bricks.
Exhorting us all the while to use non-existent public transport
As they sit comfortably with their two essential cars.

I know a place where the red brick grows
and country folk don't want what the builder sows.
Seeing through
the we-know-what-is-best-for-you politicians' pose
losing a way of life and wondering who really knows
who wants to live where the red brick grows.

ANGELUS BELL

    The Angelus bell tolls its single note.
Wheezy chested grunt then a slap as the rope is loosened.
And the bell tolls a single note
wheeze grunt dong, wheeze grunt dong
urging the faithful along.
The sun is old - up since five
the rippling breeze - it's good to be alive.
In this hot weathered bee busy flower-bursting prelude to
summer coats are cast.
Paisley two pieces, Liberty Blouses - and hats
accompany grey trousered and cream Dunn jacketed consorts
moving towards the dark hard pewed interior
to struggle with the sleep inducing sermon
and think of late lunches and lawns that must be mowed.

    The Angelus bells tolls its single note
It's heard on the eighth and sixteenth tee too
where husbands laugh and say it's 'not for you'.
A round with friends who could ask for more
Drinks and clubhouse chat - not home till four
The Angelus tolls its single note
At
Sunday-no-knicker-girls-clicking-their-high-heeled-sling-
backed-way-to-the-wine bar to lower eyes, glance through
fringes and fallen forward hair
and suddenly raise heads with gales of laughter
all the time aware
of the key jangling, volume voiced attention seeking
pint guzzling loose rugby trousered men
And the bell tolls amen.

The bell tolls Amen
And is heard in the cool curtain drawn house
Where upstairs newly bathed and perfume dabbed she knows it's twelve noon
and 'the back door is unlocked he'll be here soon'.
The girl is out till God knows when
and you're down at the club at least until four
Who could ask for more?
The opportunities are far too few
Did you hear the bell toll?
Well it wasn't for you'!

Around the Camp Fire

GAUJO BOY

    It was just past the Rufus Stone
near the ragged oak
as the sun rolled back the mist curtain
that he first saw the smoke.
Then the clustered wagons
and the group around the fire.
The women and the girls by the line
strung between two vans.
Pegging out the washing, desultory chat
that ceased as he strode forward
saying 'How do' with a smile hoping to chew the fat
and maybe cadge a mug of tea.
The smile grew broader as he noticed her
arms upraised hands full of washing.
Raven hair to the waist
an exotic beauty.
A raklie whose family would keep her chaste
for the marriage bed.
The face remained impassive as an older women uttered one sharp word
but the eyes glittered with suppressed humour
He took two paces more
and the men shortened the distance between them.
The older one in the middle spat in the fire
turned his back -cut short his friendly ploy
and the scornful words came like arrows
as he flung them
        Gaugo Boy!

He arrived early in the day
as they watched the pony traps race on the A27
and was pointedly ignored.
As they camped at Little Egypt beside the River Mole.
He appeared again and tried to talk,
this captivating soul.
He saw her grin - his heart leaped for joy.
The sister's arched eyebrows enquired, and the mother replied
     Gaujo Boy.

At Stow on the Wold he bought a van from Jemmy Lee
learned to tie a silk diklo, and was still ignored.
Camped by the circus folk at Shrewsbury
they were involved in the big fire in the night.
He was helping everywhere, struggling with all his might
to free a sticking brake and get a wagon to safety.
Bursting through the flames to get to the dog and child
who had run in after it.
Emerging with one under each arm
and scorch marks on his back.
In the morning hearing the deep voiced 'ahoy!'
Turning as the boots squelched through the swamp left by the firemen
and the father handed him a steaming mug of tea
gravely nodded and said evenly
     Gaujo Boy.

    By the time they got to Dublin and down to Galway Bay
she made her feelings plain and started to get her way.
Chatting to him easily but her mother always close.
The music drew them to the Lisdoonvarna Marriage Stakes.
His feet tapped in tune as he smiled at what was on offer
was polite but did not dance,
knowing he was watched
knowing he must not spoil his very precious chance.

He bought a Connemara mare
and sold it in June at Appleby Fair
and as a party they journeyed South.
The Romanis in convoy
and at the back the
        Gaujo Boy.

    Past the old'uns at Pooks Hill.
Over Ashdown Forest
to pass time in Storrington with Jacko and Ruby
where the couple left the talking
-   jumped the broom at Fulking.
Accepted by the Boswells, Lovells, Lees and Ruben Smith
even the Penfolds know the family he's with
do not take to outsiders
but the newborn chavvy
gives them joy
and the father is now known as
their own
        Gaujo Boy.

Glossary

Gaujo - Outsider - Non-Romany.

Diklo - Neckerchief scarf usually predominantly yellow.

Raklie - A single young Romany girl.

Chavvy - Small child.

ECUMENICAL WITH THE TRUTH

With tea and cake benevolent faces and ponderous gravity
You stood in front and addressed us at length.
 'You are too few, the walls are crumbling, ruined.
 Another Methodist Church, a newer building
 They're just like you, we counsel merging'.
You Circuit Ministers planned our future
- and looked to Canterbury for your own.

Maybe you were right, there was no other way
But you destroyed a community as surely as if
 You shelled a village in Bosnia.

GOD IS OUR REFUGE AND OUR STRENGTH

Letters on the wall around a painted cross.
Strange how the fabric lives on for the Welsh
 And we still feel the loss.

> In the early 1960s the Methodist Church pursued a policy of integrating small congregations and disposing of surplus buildings. Lind Road Methodist Church, Sutton, was sold to the Welsh Presbyterian movement. At the same time, the Methodist ministry explored the possibility of merging with the Church of England

HOUSE CLEARANCE

The May sun by its strength
penetrating the net curtains
raising the dust motes to dance to its tune.
Bringing not warmth but a reminder of a world outside.
The ebony backed hairbrushes offered
their silver initials to the shaft of light.
Conscious of the clinging hairs
but not disposed to remove the grey reminders
pausing briefly he snapped the brushes
face to face into the black sack.
To join the brown leather straps and nameless
pieces that fitted in the cardboard box
labelled Harrisons Patent Truss.
The arm bands, large collared shirts
and sundry ties, thick pyjamas and
highly polished brown shoes of the one time soldier.
Who had himself used a black sack
to dispose of his wife's shoes
and in a clinical soldierly fashion
cleared her effects out of his life
to become for the second time a widower.
In turn the hospital bundled his
possessions into one and presenting 'the list'
were surprised to hear of the missing ring.

The doughty warrior, stubborn to the last
lingered for weeks.
Plotted to escape and wrote asking to be removed.
Eventually the Great Remover obliged.

The sun for him fashioned a bright last day.
The nieces rode with the son in the car
following the hearse.

The members of the bowls club gave more respect
to the ex-member than they had when he joined them on
                                                                               the green.
Faithful to the last, the spinster friend of his wife
In black hat and boots
Waited grimly at the cemetery gate.
To see off the last of the partners
she had brought together.

The empty house seemed but a husk
to the son who had never called it home.
More so than the empty shell
viewed cautiously in the undertakers chapel
where he marvelled at the still vigorous grey hair
before tiptoeing out with a murmured 'bye Dad'.
Now the appointed guardian of the memories
listened for the joyful laugh and wished
to hear just one more time the done to death
anecdotes and time served jokes.
The empty house, redolent still of cigars and burnt
                                                                               saucepans,
contained no terrors and no life.
Try as he might it remained - empty
A reverie breaking peal at the door bell
announced that the men had arrived to clear the house.
Admitting them he carried the sack
to the boot of his car to dispose privately
of the personal bits and pieces.
'All to go Guv?'
'Yes' he replied.
Watching the hall-stand carried to the van
Remembering removing from its seat, on his fathers
                                                                              instructions,
from between the newspapers
the rolls of hoarded treasury bills

JAM AND JERUSALEM

    Fourteen years since our last meeting
You said with arms embracing joyful greeting.
At last the long delayed visit, armed with flowers
I had come to spend a few fleeting hours.

    Travelling over Tower Bridge, this time by car
I remembered the daily journey of the past
walking in the morning, trotting in the evening to
still breathing well, arrive at London Bridge
and leave for leafy Surrey - a bridge too far.
The morning air was full of city importance
The evening relief and survival.
And now a changed landscape
converted warehouses vying with old inns
offering new fare.
Everywhere the new scene still argued
the history of its roots.

    Here in your second floor salon
we ate and drank with tradition
As the moon washed over Hawksmoor's Church
and shafted light through the slatted blinds
to lend lunar power to the candlelit table
'A bomber's moon' said this old label child
and journeyed with you on a mind voyage.
We spoke of the essential evil of capitalism
(but the energy power of money).
Of the student riots of 1962
Jean-Paul Sartre, Simone de Beauvoir.
Of Moseley March and Cable Street
-     and Henry Williamson.
The International Brigade, a Spanish rehearsal.
The Guggenheim and St Ives
The ducks on our Surrey pond - all part of our lives.

    At last time to go and we waved from the balcony
to Geoff as he parked the Jag
A pot of your homemade jam and enduring gift of
                                        friendship
saw me on my way.
And your words
A night flight to arrive in Israel with the sunrise
the smell of oranges - would I join you?

Maybe
            Next Year in Jerusalem.

JOHN

I wish I had known you John.
When I was a boy you were deemed to be the devil
You were a communist.
What was it that prompted you to go and fight in Spain
For a cause that was not of your country?
You were married to my cousin.
I knew my cousin and I knew your children,
But you I never knew.
Now, with age, I can think of justice,
of liberty and a long, continuing fight
and battles long gone.
Where are you now?
I wish I'd known you, John.

COUSIN PETER

Cousin Peter is a quiet man.
Always transparent his virtues are easily available
his failings few.
Steadfast through the years in his enthusiastic
pursuit of what were boyhood hobbies
the trains and buses have become more sophisticated
with the use of computer based technology.
The backdrop of village and sidings more skilfully
created and the layout far transcends his boyhood dreams.

His extensive collection of music from the
dance band days, like his models available
to be shared.
Steadfast to his marriage vows
a considerate loving spouse
proudly displaying still the wedding photographs.
A considerate neighbour giving regular cheer to all
faithfully in his friendship and support.
Well mannered and courteous looking only for a similar
return,
not offended but hurt when others are less gracious.
Cousin Peter is a quite man.
May God help England to continue to fashion his like.

TALK OF THE DEVIL

'It's the devil's own job.'
Her son-in-law's voice carried from the kitchen.
The washing machine had flooded the floor.
She had apparently blocked something.
These days he seemed to blame her more and more.
For losing the mobile phone they'd inflicted on her.
For locking herself out, for forgetting her daughter's birthday
and the outing on the Bluebell Railway he'd arranged.
It could happen to anyone and they were always arranging
                                             something.
In a way she was quite relieved Joan had insisted she stay in
                                             the lounge
and leave everything to them.
In the garden the bluetits burst through the shafts of sunshine
and popped into the nesting box emerging quickly to
Repeat the exercise and feed the nestlings.
Rose petals drifted onto the border and the lilies quivered on
the pond.
Indoors sheltered from the breeze, conscious of the ticking
clock beside
the sparkling cut-glass jar in which her husband used to keep
his tobacco
She felt cosy but somehow isolated.

    Lately it had been one thing after another.
She'd mistimed the oven, cremated the meat and the
whole place smelt for days, the oven took forever to clean,
oh, and the saucepan boiled dry and riveted the potatoes
                                                 inside it.

In the town, road-works caused diversion signs.
One said 'pedestrians' and following it took her for miles
thoroughly lost she had to ask a kindly stranger to guide her
 home
even then for a brief while the houses in the street looked
 unfamiliar.
In the supermarket foolishly she'd forgotten her purse
and had a big altercation with a stupid chit of a girl at
 checkout.
So, excited and stirred up, she momentarily
forgot her address
and the girl would not give her time to think
but gabbled incessantly with no punctuation so that not a
 word
Was decipherable.
One thing after another, maybe Rob was right,
 the devil's own job.

As a tiny child she had been threatened by her mother that
for her naughtiness the devil would come and take her away.
Terrified for days she eventually asked her grandmother for
confirmation
and was told in a kindly way 'not this time.'
As a young girl attending a strict Baptist Church she learned
 not to blaspheme
and not to use the word devil in everyday conversation -
as Rob just had.
Sometimes recently lying in bed in the lonely quiet house
she had wondered
when it was time
 - Pray it would be quick - .
If Jesus would come for her or would it be the Other.
The Other seemed to have several names, which would he use
Satan, Lucifer, Beelzebub, Mephistophiles, Archontes
or Old Nick.

Recently there had been talk of giving up the house.
It really was too much, so hard for her to cope
move to a nice retirement home
have company and not be alone
enjoy the food provided, someone else to do the chores
a nice bright clean room of her own
and they would come and visit.

Monday the man came and re-did the kitchen floor.
Tuesday Dr Davis poked his head around the door.
Wednesday the estate agent pushed and prodded,
measured and talked earnestly with Rob.
    God knows what it was all about.
Thursday they left her alone and she had a good rest.
Friday The Devil came
    And his name was Alzheimers.

ACHTUNG SPITFIRE

    Towering over the check shirt stacked gondola
prominent nose surmounted by the green corduroy cap
comfortable in tweed jacket and cavalry twills
one arm bearing a short gabardine coat
the other shepherding the small spouse counter-wards
to dive upon the helpful assistant.
A man who will not take nonsense from Marks and Sparks.

    'The woolly zip up - what do you call it?
Can you get it in my size!'
Proudly the spouse asserts 'He needs it for Golf.'
Voice dragged past the chino's my spirits rise.
Golf! Oh Golf - can this be so!
A confidant man successful at retirement leisure and shopping.

    In the school playground the boy who became the man
had difficulty keeping up.
He, tall beyond his years
we more agile dusty ruffians played fighter planes
and straffed the angular shoulders and descended on
the outstretched scarecrow arms protruding from
the bean pole body that smelt strongly of
grey flannel and mid-morning milk.
'Heinkel Harrington! Tat tat tat tat tat!
Lie down you're done! We've shot you down!
Spitfires win! Tat tat tat tat tat!'
The battle ceased at end of play-time bell
- to resume on the morrow with more break-time hell.

National Service permanent camp was
naturally Fighter Command H.Q.
Observing me in the mess he sought me out
and told me what he had to do.
Newly arrived he was full of highly technical talk.
Suffering the amused irony of my slick companions
as they drifted away I too preferred to walk.
He still had difficulty keeping up.

Weight and muscle now flesh the once puny frame,
as does the confident perhaps not too pleasant attitude
of one who <u>will</u> get his way.
A man who knows the game
A man who can keep up.
Yet from all the M and S choice
- see his hackles begin to rise
- they hav'nt got the woolly thing available in his size.
I wondered if - in that crowded store
I could dissipate his ire
and cause him to fall upon the floor
- by yelling out that cry of yore
Achtung! Achtung Spitfire!

L'ALGERIE FRANCAIS

      The off licence dilemma moved me from shelf to shelf
Studying the racks arranged by country
suffocating in descriptive wine speak
drowning in Shiraz, Syrah and Merlot.
New world wine men teaching old houses
                        to blur the boundaries
to an acceptable Friday night level.
To choose a wine whose price denotes wealth
or a cheap and cheerful?
When, under 'Other Countries'
a thought entered my head.
Whatever happened to Algerian Red?

      Do you remember the days when we talked forever
and were convinced that we all of us were terribly clever?
The Friday night sessions around the fire.
Girls in stilettos short dresses and beads
acknowledging poverty and the workers' needs.
Boys in black sweaters and Henry V hair.
Chasing the conversation striving to remember what was said.
All the time fuelled on Algerian Red.

      Strong coffee and Gauloises
laughing at Flook and Trog
exchanging the latest Kerouac listening to Thelonius Monk
                        and getting drunk
on Algerian Red.

      Thomas churning out page after page of his novel
fuelled on speed and Algerian Red.
Mo' the drama queen, full of tuition
ambition, audition
and regular sips of Algerian Red.

Copious draughts of
Poets and Beats music and treats
That Was the Week That Was. . . . .
Saturday night slipping into Sunday morning
because we had been led
to open another bottle of . . . . . Algerian Red.

On Monday leaping aboard the London train
Already gathering speed
Collapsing into a seat nursing a concrete head
Cemented hard with Algerian Red.

      We changed and we moved and gave up the dance
the crusade was over, hung up the lance
and discovered the faults of the man called Kennedy.

James changed from dental mechanic to city clerk
married an ex-prostitute - but it wasn't a lark
the charcoal grey suit and rolled umbrella
just made him a totally different feller
full of respectability.
Ban-the-bomb-Val was arrested but joined the Civil Service.
Linda met Ron, moved and pushed a pram on the front at
Worthing.
Dudley switched from theology to law
we promised to stay in touch and slowly heard no more.

      The years have gone by and the world now spins
faster.
Yesterday looks good against tomorrow's disaster
and memory stays shoulder to shoulder as a constant companion.
How fare you now brave comrades in arms
are some of you rich - and some of you dead?
If we meet now perchance does age bring new charms
and do we remind one another - of Algerian Red!

DOWN AT JOHNNY IDLE'S

Crinkly grey eyes set in the tragic/comedy face of a clown
living in a small house on the edge of town.
The smoke rising cardinal fashion from the chimney
seen above the trees on the downhill path from Potters Wood.
The gang wend their separate ways
for another session at Johnny Idle's.

Two old sunken sofas two arm chairs and a garden bench
enable the company to take their ease.
Fred-the-Fish, the unlistening man's expert on local politics
talks of the might-be road.
'We'll be left with a deserted town -
all to get to Chi in Ten minutes.'
The pause for breath
let's John-the-Clock in
'It'll be peaceful'
'It'll be death!'
Big Tony 'You should know!'
'They're all dead on your slab - all on show!'
'I brought some nice haddock -
Johnny's at it now.'
'Time for a pre-prandial?'
A carefully modulated enquiry from Crispin Sheepe
antique man of repute.
Thrown close to Sol dor Pam by the sofa's exhausted sagging.
A picture of studied elegance from the lemon breast pocket
hanky
to the slightly scuffed suede chucka boots.
Hand on his sleeve 'You're opening the wine, what a treasure.'
Pam's cool blue gaze shows she's got his measure.
Close cropped hair managing to look butch but exude sex.
Her little shop has teddy's gifties and throws,
jewellery, china, postcards - oh anything goes
at Sol dor Pam's.

The circulating wine is crossed
by the anti-clockwise well buttered bread and haddock.
Served by Dave Books.
He and Johnny in tandem
act as the cooks.
Contrapuntal rhythms of conversation.
simultaneous disparate topics help to heat the alchemic mix.
That is an evening at Johnny Idel's

Matilda May the florist asks Pam for
a further supply of flowers preserved in fancy glass containers.
Big Tony talks of the catalogue he will print
for John-the-Clock, who would prefer his wares not to be
stated - and in turn talks to Dave of last night's Channel Four
- who gave up TV long ago for more quality time.
and Crispin raising his voice talks of retainers
to Father Grogan
(but knows this is a subject they will all follow.)
'The little picture you adored
The Hare in the Hollow.'
'Glad to get thirty five from your friend Tom.
The artist Michael Jinks now v. in demand
would gladly give four hundred for its like again.'
'Ah, Tom disposed of it to the late Miss Rawling.'
'And I got it from her niece,' adds Tone,
'and let it go for a small consideration' -
'To me" smiles Pam 'but, alas, it had to go.
The guttering and the roof repairs you know.'
Bartered it as payment.

From the kitchen emerges a coffee cup
and dunking biscuit about to fall
its owners smile makes him eight feet tall.
"Did I hear found hundred?"
and isn't that just
the luck of Johnny Idle.

HOME COUNTIES SARAH

Sarah was a bright girl, her headmistress always said and
she determined they would go far when she and Richard wed.
Swiftly they forsook Worcester Park
for the far horizons of Dorking.
As swiftly discarding the old friends and neighbours.
They were comfortable in Dorking.

Richard had a company car
and drove himself to and from the station.
Sarah kept house, looked after the children,
Constantly 'updated' and got to know lots of
little men who came and did
the electric's, the decorating and the replacement windows.
After a while they saw that Dorking had become suburban
and the people had no style.
The house at Weybridge was bigger and nicer in every way.
St. Johns was a good school and the boy was down for
Charterhouse.
Au pairs came and went, it really was a trial.
Sarah joined the tennis club, had coffee with the girls
and sallied to the hairdresser's for highlights in her curls.
She got on two committee's, for getting on she had the knack.
Driving her Peugeot
with the sticker: 'Hold Back - Baby on Board' in the back.
Richard came home and fell asleep after dinner.

They crossed the Thames to Marlow and Sarah knew they had
                                                               arrived.
Pickford's provided packers and un-packers
the family spent the night at The Bear at Woodstock.
With this little bit of cosseting the move they had survived.
The children spent time on the river.
Sarah changed to the Volvo estate

and shared the school run with blonde patrician Claire.
Claire's solicitor husband, James, was jolly, hearty, and he and Richard
watched rugby together.
Dining out at the Compleat Angler and other prestigious establishments.
Entertaining at home with the aid of the new kitchen.
Joining the bridge circle, Sarah's life was busy
and her cup full.
At Christmas she bedecked the reception hall with holly
And the waits sang to the guests.
Richard took to coming home and falling asleep before dinner.

In the New Year Sarah sent out a lively family newsletter
little knowing what was round the corner.
Richard got his big promotion but had to move to Manchester.
Sarah had become a leading light in 'The Maidenhead
                                                                               Players'.
Gave a performance to end all performances - and refused to
                                                                                            go.
The parting was bitter and acrimonious.
Forced to move to something less commodious
she chose High Wycombe.
Where supported by friends in the same boat
she spent time in the local wine bar
talking one another up, getting that *frisson* of excitement
when a twenty-five and muscular man paused long
                                                                              on entering.
Sadly he was not struck by the forty-something short skirts on
                                                                                      offer
But was trying to remember if he had locked the front door.
She has the children but they holiday with their father
and his new wife in Andorra and Antigua
before returning to this lost-her-way mother-carer
who they call with no concealment 'draggie Sarah'.

HOLIDAYS

January and February were mild
and wet and no one
spoke of holidays.
March arrived and a colleague
disappeared on a short break.
April produced Easter
and people went away
telephones were unanswered
and I lived in an empty world.
May and June were full of
comings and goings
bargain breaks and continuous
accounts of places seen
and food consumed.
July led into August
school holidays took people away
and the office and the streets
seemed deserted.
Rather than stay and be thought lonely
I booked for the festival
and was busy for a week
making no new friends.
September started warm
and was lovely.
You arrived
and I got a life.

NIGHT VISION

-1-

Stealthing through the woods at owl hoot time
-      I heard a whisper.
Motionless I waited.
Hearing the wind whistle through the trees
as though it were on the shore and playing with the waves.
Different somehow.
Motionless I remained for it was not this I had heard.
Aware of the pale moon shafting through the mainly leafless
                                                                                          trees
their rich canopy now under foot,
detecting the creak of branch
and sigh of dying timber
back to trunk senses a-quiver -
Motionless I stood aware it was not this sound..
A small animal broke its sentry pose and moved through the
                                                                                    undergrowth.
Motionless I and still very loath
to believe I was mistaken.

At last I ventured forward
emboldened, crossed the clearing
found the path and stopped on hearing
something up ahead.
Too heavy for animal, more like man
suppressing my instincts as I almost turned and ran -
Motionless I crouched
below the eye line.

Then irritated I rose and hurried towards the noise
hearing it nearer I hurried more
following it closer as we turned off the path
and wove in and out of the sturdy trees.
Suddenly silence - then it was there again
way off to the right.
Hot in pursuit careless of my footing
a tree root brought me to my knees.
Up front born on the frosty air it sounded like a faint laugh.
Then chilling quiet, and nothing as I edged closer
remembering my woodcraft.
Then it was I heard him way behind me.

Is this what comes of poaching in another mans' woods?

-2-

What game are we playing
hoodman blind or hunt the fox
who is hunter and who the quarry?
Who will catch the prize and whose ears get the box?
Circling one another striving for position.
Will it come down to who is in best condition,
who can keep up this vigorous pace.
Then as my heart pounded and sought to leap out of my chest
accompanied by the faint whine of a distant lorry way out on
the road

We came face to face.

I court not further pain
I'll not go back
And neither will I speak of this again
For I have seen -
                 The Hooded Man.

TOAD IN BLUE JEANS

    Heavy hand displaying rings
firmly grasping a box of Snow White sweets
an impulsive thought for children's treats
knowing he might share one or four
passing the box round more and more.

    Standing in the so English queue in
the village paper shop
Blue jeans stiff from lack of use
encase the XL rear and the sturdy legs.
The forward thrusting belly displaying the Argyle
patterned sweater.
The commuting hardened incisive stance confirms he's better
than the locals getting in the way
of a dyed in the wool city-man.
His weekend given up to accompany the family
and stay with mother-in-law.
Escaping the mother-daughter verbal ballet
to visit the village shops and walk the kids along the shore
'I don't suppose you have the Investor's Chronicle?'
he asks on being served, disconcerted to be directed
to the rack- and forced to buy - but not to read
a publication he did not really need.
    Toad has come to visit.

    Later in the Fox his nut brown tones
will soar above the rest of the conversation
as his Hampstead casual dress stands out
from the rugby shirts, yachting jackets and Henry's tweeds.
Offering to buy a round to the company's consternation.
Using this as the excuse to inform them at length
of the work left undone.
the boredom and trials and tribulations that befall
this dutiful son in law.
    'Granada's up and so's Savoy, Mirror Group's down
but listen boy, now's the time to pile into food'.
Dickens ironic 'You believe in it then' slips by.
Draining his glass, pausing at the door to cry
loudly 'Back to Colditz' he exits.

    The empty space vacuum-like draws them together
and conversation moves to womanising two-timing John.
Tray full of glasses Jan puts down her load.
Cry's 'My sister was right, you are a toad!'
The focus of attention is directed at John
general merriment as he reply's, 'no - he's just gone!'

WOOLLEN HAT

    Huddled at a window table
they linger over lunch.
Working hard at the relationship was my hunch.
Both in their twenties.
He sups regularly at his beer
talking earnestly free hand beating the air to emphasize a
                                                                         point
sober in his endeavour.
Well built, strong hands, open necked shirt and comfortable
                                                                         jacket.
She has an elfin-look, animatedly gamin.
The large luminous eyes almost overwhelm the porcelain pale
                                                                         face.
Stick thin in jeans and zipped up fleece.
Woollen knitted hat pulled tight around the ears
she laughs, cuts his flow of words altering his conversational
                                                                         pace.

    Finishing the last mouthful he pushes his plate away
as though terminating a skirmish, returning to what he had to
                                                                         say.
Learning back grinning with amusement she assays a one
                                                                         liner,
then controls the talk, altering the temperature
lightening it with frothy witty conversation
one hand outlining an airy parabola
the un-ringed slender fingers palely naked.
Producing a notebook from his pocket he starts to write.
Tenderly, smiling, she shuts the notebook tight.
Can money be the sticking point between them?

    The people seated at the table by the fire leave
allowing the unscreened heat
to mix with the warmth of the sun through the window
basking the couple in a temperate golden glow.
Coaxing a smile from her man
she sips from her glass, her plate largely untouched before
                                                              her.
Effervescent with humour she makes him laugh.
Confident as they rise her mind in the ascendant knowing she
                                                              has won
scratches the back of her head dislodging the woollen hat.
    Showing what the chemo has done.

SOMETHING IN THE CITY

    'Life's a bitch, and then you die'
-        so-called friends and their incessant cry,
as they shaft you and betray you and you wonder why.
As false a statement as their hearty telephoned 'Hi!
It's Peter or Felicity, Will or Bee,
'I thought I'd call - just to see,
if you're alright.'

    You gave your word and they gave theirs.
You stood by yours and they broke theirs
invented reasons and found ways
to do you down, these protégés.
You trained them and you honed them,
your word your bond, an inherited tradition
- when they were short of stock covered their position.
You needed help but it was always then,
they were in dollars when it should be in yen.

    Damning with faint praise they went behind your back
and made it seem so clear
they had saved you from a disastrous year
and stole your bonus.
Little by little, more by more
they showed there were too many for the team of four
hinted you'd had a long run, would like to call it a day,
ease down and smell the roses, draw your pay.

You still rise early but spend the day at home
dull, as the hours crawl by broken only by the telephone.
Callers who believe everything goes, to those who dare
to break their word as lightly as a leaf,
to steal another's job is not behaving like a thief.

'We wish you well
and thanks to you are swell,
found it easy with the protection
of what you had crafted - your connection.
But look, old sport
please don't count on our support,
love to help you - really try
- but life's a bitch and then you die.'

SING DUSTY SING

      Why Dusty why did you throw it all away.
We didn't care if you were straight or gay.
We only wanted you to sing and not go away.
Do you remember Dusty those evenings at Queenie Watts
When the whole world came and partied,
and Queenie did her stuff,
and the males in attendance were never enough
for our Dusty.
Farson came and Boothroyd came,
the Krays looked in the door.
You sang to our persuasion, we loved you more and more.

      America proved a wasteland.
You came back to a comeback
and sang with a band.
The Pet Shop Boys needed you
to give them a helping hand.
But Dusty we needed you as a star, not an also ran.
Someone to fall in love with, The Son of a Preacher Man.
If there was a last performance we weren't around to see.
So, Mary O'Brien, our Dusty, sing once more
                              for them and me.

O'GRADY

She came out of his office
Stood showing broad feet and thick ankles
'Mr Pumphret says you're to get all your bank statements.
Mr Pamphret says you're to produce all the invoices
Mr Pamphret says to 'phone in ten days for an appointment.'
'Like O'Grady I said. . . . . .'

The childhood game recalled
when you had to do whatever O'Grady said
'O'Grady says you're to stand on your head.'
'O'Grady says you're to hop on one leg to the end of the road.'
O'Grady never spoke in person but issued commands through
a third party
invariably a puffed up with importance fat be-spectacled
child.
      I never liked O'Grady.

SMALL BUSINESS

     He wrote to me yesterday
out of the blue - so unexpected -
and this is what he had to say.

     'I am writing to advise you the bank
has asked me to take on a new role,
and with immediate effect my colleague Simon Brand
will look after your accounts.'
So I'm to call him if I need a hand.

     Addressing me familiarly although we never met
he was not like a proper
Bank Manager in days of old,
who lunched us, invited us to functions
and nurtured our accounts -
until the powers that be, broke the mould.
Moving all the managers miles away
to an area office
leaving us with promoted clerks who had the title
but no authority to manage.

All his training and experience have qualified him to fail
at the new role.
Forced to take up the poisoned chalice of Financial Services
and try to sell the Banks products to
ever wary and sceptical customers.
With failure inevitable downsizing 'Have to let you go.'
A taste of what it's like outside
'they have taken away your comfortable ride.'

     He signed the letter for the last time
Small Business Manager.
Well,
he's Small Potatoes now.

RETURN TICKET

      The grass is weathered now in the field
that lies beyond the back garden vegetables
and runs up hill toward the heath.
Summer's lease is slipping and Autumn's bitter sweet
cornucopia hovers.
The dog walking track runs diagonally across the field
at the top to yield
entry to the spruce flanked dank and overshadowed avenue
that releases the resin and pine perfumed drunk
onto the heath

      This favoured spot, this paradise
with acres of thick bracken tall enough to conceal a man
and little tracks that lead past clumps of young silver birch
and luscious blackberries and dipping suddenly, can
in a trice,
drop you three feet down and all awry

      Early morning walks across the health to buy the eggs
and languorous afternoons sharing lunch, conversation and
books
with friends.
The pleasures of youth taken gratefully in a time that
never ends.
Yet somehow slipped away.

Every detail, every smell contrived to etch the memory
and fire the ambition to go back.
Perhaps the spruce have fallen and the heath gone
with rows of houses where once the tracks ran.
Perhaps it all still survives, enjoying the changing seasons.
A return visit justified by the heart with a thousand reasons,
will confirm one day
- and yet - how came this dream -
when I know that things are not as they seem.
Knowing there were no back garden vegetables
and the field did not exist
in Paradise, a whole lifetime away.

UP ON A VISIT

She had difficulty boarding the train
but a kind man leaned down, hoisted Baby up
and made it all right again.
Wanting to recall the once familiar stations
as the train lurched its way
she was too busy with Baby
expecting people to smile
as they squeezed past the buggy,
but few did.
The barriers at Victoria were difficult
but on the bus she told Baby she was oh so pretty
as they swayed and lurched from Victoria to the City.
Arriving as she had planned at lunch time
she was soon in her old office.

    The cries of recognition and cheery greeting,
the cluster of girls around Baby
made her heart warm with joy
as she had expected.

Chatting to her special friends Big Liz and Jayne
and the others hovering on the brink
made her feel the office was just the same.
They made cooing noises and hoisted Baby up
onto a desk, and were surprised to learn her weight.
Mr Wayland had just slipped out but would be back in a
while.
His new P.A. - her replacement, Angela - was introduced,
nodded briskly with a porcelain fixed smile
and left for her own office
all pin striped trouser suit and efficiency.
Liz explained,
'He got her from Maine-Tucker' (who ever they might be)
'She pretty well ran the office and was a hard cased B.'

'What have we here!' exclaimed Mr Wayland
with exuberant good cheer.
Tickling Baby under the chin.
Busy as always, he was so pleased to see them
but had to be excused to make an important special call
before lunch.

There was a general coming and going
as people procured sandwiches and ate them at their desks.
Not even Liz thought she might be hungry - in need of a bite.
They were excited over her visit, it really was alright
she reasoned.
She spoke of Baby and all her funny little ways.
They talked of clubbing and booking foreign holidays.
Gradually the crowd thinned
as the girls settled down to an afternoons mouse work.
'Oh dear', she must be leaving, the clock told ten to three.
'Come and see us soon' 'Maybe,'
she smiled, knowing she wouldn't
knowing they didn't care about Baby.

WINDOWS

I'm looking for a clear window
she said.
Mine revealed insect smears and a tiny delicate web
of fly entrapment.
In search of a plain view I walked to the High Street
past the church whose stained glass windows
threw back the suns rays in dazzling shafts of light
that shielded the interior
making me see as through a glass darkly
perceiving only in part
a window of hope.

   I remembered Peter that morning
half turning from the w.c.
To see in the cloakroom mirror an image of his father.
A window of reflectability.
The grocers windows were masked
by large banners proclaiming special prices.
The window of the Independent Financial Advisors
remained obscure.
Cloaked in cobwebs of deception
a window barred.

   She telephoned to say
on Tuesday, she had a clear window.
It rained all day and my view was opaque.

POST

The Post is bad the ancient cried,
leaning on his stick.
Pausing by his side, 'It is, it is' I replied.
'It used to come at half-past eight
but now it's always, always late,
usually it's half past one
and if short of staff
then we wait until the double shift is done.'
Developing the theme,
'At Christmas time it's cards in the hedge
and then we get some idiot's pledge,
of increased efficiency, more productivity,
staff and night train axing
more money spent, and it's you we're taxing
so we are partners in the grand venture
to get the mail promptly to your door.'
Postcodes matter - you know the score.
(So how do I get my neighbour's mail?
and mine goes on some torturous trail
around the district?)
In Victoria's reign three deliveries a day were commonplace
now hold Saturday's till Monday is often the case.

The ancient screwed up his eyes
and pointed with his stick
took a long pause
then,
'See how the gate has dipped and is hard to shut,
it's not held up any longer you can see the cause
- the post is bad.

San Jabango Days was intended as a precursor to a series of children's stories concerning a boy with a fertile imagination. Horace was the name of the caterpillar and Oswald his pet tortoise

SAN JABANGO DAYS

Do you remember now, how the sun shone all the time
scattering happiness like leaves upon us all.
A gilded life of privilege
that held us all in thrall.
The big box kite you loved to fly,
and tying the string to the handlebars of your bicycle
you would pedal for miles by the shores edge,
tanned by the sun and polished by the balmy sea breeze.

   Red and yellow was the kite, the colours of the state
used on the passports and the bunting at Christmas
and displayed on the flags so proudly flown at the
Presidential palace.
Three when he was home and one when he was elsewhere
in far San Jabango.

   You kept a tortoise, collected caterpillars, climbed the trees,
learned tennis and kept the servants busy as bees
providing drinks and meals and clean safari suits.
Long and active days, the sun high in the sky by five-thirty,
breakfast on the veranda where in the cool of the evening
we would again gather for bedtime drinks and chatter
enjoying the roosting bird's evensong.
Your little bivouac tent on the lawn
first drew his attention
but it was a surprise to us all
when President Pinsker came to call
on us in far San Jabango

   He took a shine to you, my son,
organised visits and excursions.
Found you a small enough pony
fit and able to keep up with the others
and showed you the ancient temple surmounting the hill
inhabited now only by deer that come to eat the young shoots
that grow between the lonely stones.
From this eyrie, this vantage point, you looked down
upon the city and watched the little train
puff its way past the coastal cantrefs
to the port where the big ships berthed.

Concerts and banquets in the palace
you had them all and ate off gold plate,
drank from red goblets
confident little man discussing books and good food
but never able to persuade him that peanut butter
was food for the gods.

   In the courtyard by the big fountain
President Pinsker would practice open government
and sit in judgement.
He had made for you a smaller version of his throne
that you might learn.
Sometimes asked for advice and found your pronouncements
droll,
hands beating rhythmically like wings across the ample
stomach
as he heaved with laughter.

      Mysterious whisperings in the candlelit cathedral

     A little attentive ear claimed his in turn
and when
the insurgents came.
The first Sir Dagric held the stair
with flashing blade
flanked by
Oswald, with the tortoise shield
and deadly axe that he would yield
so dextrously.
Horace who seemed to have many legs
so swiftly did he dart in and out protecting Dagric's right
and pushing back the mob.
Keeping the President safe till the army came,
then it was a different game
and soon over.

     Back here the climate is colder,
we grow a little older
and are cheered when,
once a year, in blossom time
on 'Dagric's Day',
a single red gold bloom arrives
to remind us of those whose lives
we shared in far San Jabango.

TIME

Yesterday there was another yesterday
before that another and another.
If you add them all together
they are us.
Yesterday is a day you cannot change
a day that is now memory.
So if all our life is memory
how do we shape it?
By making sure tomorrow and tomorrow
become the best yesterdays.
For they are us.

ICARUS ABOVE STEYNING BOWL

    A clumsy shuffle, ungainly leap
to rise above the dogs and two pole-wielding, posing
Sunday strollers
to hang momentarily then swiftly soar
above the singing larks.
Are you buzzard like rising on a thermal
or harnessing the wind commanding it to carry you
where you will
instructing it to stay with you, play with you
and not be still.

    Do you sail past Wiston Barn
skirt Chanctonbury pass Sullington
to gaze on the deer in proud Parham's Park.
Does the wind deafen you
can you revel in the views below
cocooned within your goggles -
obscured from it all
content to hang and glide,
does the wind hold you in its thrall?

    Do you go where the wind listeth
slip past Cowbottom Hovel,
ignore Sompting's Templar Church
loop round to Beeding Hill
and work back to the Bowl.
Do you have dihedral at the wind tips.
can you ride the wind like valkyrie
speeding on your way
are you warm-ed in the sun
and God like, unanswerable to none?

THE POETS WORE GREY SUITS

-I-

The lads from the Eagle were the first to arrive
relaxed and natural, kicked the evening alive
followed closely by the girls from the gospel choir.
The city boys came to the party in
their Friday dress-down gear
stuffing their mouths and filling the room with raucous hoots.
And the Poets wore grey suits.

The teachers wore their usual unwashed jeans.
Social workers in sombre brown
gave handshakes and exhibited the habitual frown
trying to workout the politics of the evening.
Students with hungry mouths eyed with disbelief
the teachers and social workers they would in turn become.
The I.T. girls made a mid-room huddle, breath-sharing afraid
not to be so near.
Up and coming glory solicitors vied with the
hairdressers and bought from the designers of the year.
Positioned by the bar as though they had grown roots
the Poets wore grey suits.

Imposed connections from the Rotary Club
overwhelmed by
advertising exec's with mouths in fixed smiles
like hungry piranhas
eyes masked by their Dolce and Gabbana's.
Eyed by two rude boys
Hissy Missy talked her sibilant way
to the chocolate fountain
and an evenings overdosed bliss.

-II-

    Flirty Herti
in a froth of white lace above a short black skirt
making her usual late entrance, pausing to be seen
accepting champagne with the air of a queen.
Mindful of her manners she
stalks her high heeled sheer stockinged predatory way
and greets the host like a long lost lover.

    Johnny Idle in the money, Johnny Idle - what a honey!
One big win and he doesn't care Johnny Idle loves to share.
Smiling, smiling standing and seeing
a host of people he doesn't know.
A pack of ligers who fail to recognise the host
and tomorrow will pass by without wave or nod
this man of integrity who impoverished often has never
                                                                                        begged
and now in his wealth eyes them with benign amusement.

    Eventually the hot free filling free swilling free everything
evening implodes, fragments, and folk start to go
leaving some on chairs who on being shaken will decide to
                                                                                                waken
and maintain they were conscious all the while.
Johnny Idle waves and with a wide smile
watches those with ties askew and shades slipping below one
                                                                                               eye depart.
In the cool entrance lobby glasses in hand
listening to some cars' farewell toots
stand

    The Poets who wore grey suits.

JOBS AND JAM

Should the State serve the Citizens
or the Citizens serve the State?
There is a new religion which we truly, truly hate.

We have read the doctrine and understand the aim
to educate us to be dependable and very, very tame.
The Slave Trade was abolished in 1807
but total servants of the State are less
than Slaves who served one master,
not hordes of humourless grey-faced
wey-faced invigilators
who delight in checking for compliance.
To be compliant is to yield
and be snivellingly obliging.
Parrot the mantra, keep nose and feet clean
be eager to report the shortcomings of others
and never feel mean.
If we are extra diligent there may be a job for us
within a government department -
if we do not make a fuss.
Government - central or local - or serving as a quango
it doesn't matter, just learn to tango
to the State tune
and reduce the unemployment 'figures'.

We may fake it, shake it, spurn it,
but never, ever, make it
our bounden duty to bear the yoke of State servitude
and be politically correct.
No. We will say what we think and call a spade a spade
and not play to the ever changing rules they have made.
For modern Britain's Slavery smacks of Knavery.

A CHANCE ENCOUNTER

It was very unexpected.
The show was on, the house was full;
Cleo Laine and John Dankworth still drawing fans from near
and far.
As the music flowed John's tapping feet
seemed to summon another to follow the beat.
In the full to capacity venue in the hot and crowded row
you joined us.
As my mind was fully occupied by the music
I became aware you were by my side.
Companionly close.

Still the same fresh faced vibrant twenty three year old
I almost expected to hear the apology of a latecomer.
Surely memory should be blunt after all these years
so many must have forgotten your name and that time of tears
yet the clothes you wore were as clear
as your grin and the humour filled blue eyes
your presence at the concert
was physical.

By now you could perhaps be a grandfather
A success in life, comfortable in your achievements.
Certainly still a character.
Would we have stayed in contact; would we have stayed close
or would the paths we chose taken us apart?
I do not think so.
Not a David and Jonathan relationship
but a friendship that always had room for others
who were glad to be in your company.
Neither of us leaders yet seemingly by default we led.
When the water claimed you, put you amongst the dead
a line was drawn, a chapter finished.
But our chapter was your life.

    I could say so much more
but why elaborate - it's all been said before.
You had gone by the time I gained the exit door
spilling out with the rest of the happy host.
So; thanks for your company,

                    Brian.

                 my friendly ghost.

TWO LOVES

It was the mistress first who made him and then the wife.
The wife who made him forget,
brought out his light-hearted side.
Made every day a joy, gave him a son
and filled him with pride.
Broke his heart
and left all too short a life.

He returned to the mistress
but with the babe it was not easy
and he soon returned to a barren house
a job and daily grind, chaos and beneath the inadvertent feet
more and more crunching toys.
In-laws taking over the house and noise
more and more noise.

The decades-claiming job
took him from young man to retiree
and through it all
everyday he thought of the mistress who had claimed him
and in distance never let him go but held him
inexorably in thrall.
He could smell her unique perfume,
remembered all her ways.
In cold and damp, in the suburb parched summer sun
he saw her daily, remembered her, but never went back.

Troopships no longer ply to Bombay.
The fishing fleet no longer brings potential wives
to stay with relatives
and be paraded at church, bridge and dances.
The sights sounds and creaking punkahs
were bitter sweet
and everyday, to his dying day,
he remembered his first love
his great love
his love for India.

Over the Hills and Far Away

A VITAL PIECE OF EVIDENCE

In the land of the local shows
they were always the chief contenders.
Sometimes he would do his rival down
but of recent years Harris had started to manoeuvre
and when <u>he</u> was in onions
King Harris would be carrots
avoiding the head to head keeping his crown.
This year <u>he</u> held back
waiting till he by devious means gained the moment of clarity
and learned the Harris chosen specialty.

Entry delayed until the very last
he would reveal his hand learning from the past.
In the meantime nurturing, specialty feeding
fine camel brush titillating, impregnating
rearing the 1st in Class
and Best in Show.
He knew, he knew, he knew, he was ready to go
and would be first, first, first.
Only to be thwarted by her who should be cursed, cursed, cursed.

    The fires of passion long quenched the marriage
was not bedded in companionship.
No mutual interests held them together
the cement that tied was her constant barbs and bitter quips
till manoeuvred thrust told her she's scored.
Yet he constantly silently ignored
the storms and heavy weather.
In public the acid tongue
would whip him as she, arm round him, clung
smiled and called him darling
and he smiled and maintained his stance.

-II-

With thoughts benign he entered the greenhouse
to behold her, glee transparent, scissors in one hand
and in the other
his prize cucumber, best in show, Harris downer no more.
'The girls from the W.I. are here tomorrow for tea
   -   this will do just nicely, with plenty more
you don't begrudge it little me.'
In the ashes of defeated ambition
for a matter of seconds hatred boiled over, reached fruition
them with no word spoken he turned on his heel
entered the house, donned a jacket
and left for the pub -

   Returning at length entering the house, he called
and heard only the hall clock.
In half an hour, tossing the newspaper aside,
he strolled into the garden
and beheld her
face down lifeless in the greenhouse.

   The rest of the day passed in a blur.
The 'services' came and the police stayed
waiting for a man called soco
who dusted, took fingerprints and photographs
the police surgeon came,
examined and finally arranged to release her.
They were most considerate, local people like him
and arranged that Inspector Mansfield -
who he knew as Maurice
would with sergeant interview him tomorrow around three.

-III-

Easy chairs in the lounge
easy conversation.
'No sign of forced entry,
perhaps an opportunist invasion through the side entry.
Not expecting her - wrong place, wrong time.
Silenced with a blunt instrument, abnormally thin skull
nothing taken - must have panicked.'
Tea and sympathy.
No heart for The Show -
not sure he would ever have another go.
Please do not worry.
They would eventually get their man
combing the district for the blunt instrument
no doubt discarded in a hurry
a vital piece of evidence, no doubt have prints
'Evidently' he said
as they devoured with relish
the thick buttered cucumber sandwiches
'Evidently.'

HOME JAMES

     Home James and don't spare the horses!
Tonight is our curry night.
We will order several dishes
for we know how to do things right.
We have forsaken Giuesppi's Italian
in favour of the Bengal Night.
With papadoms to crunch
and warm naan to munch
we'll study the menu hard
and order our several dishes
for we know how to do things right.
A portion of this and a portion of that
and two of where my thumb is.
The menu is vast but we are not fazed
at our knowledge of Indian you'd be amazed.
We'll order what suits me and Carla.
Madras is v. hot
-    so let's have our favourite chicken masala.
we'll not have the beer or the lager
but do it in style with a nice chardonnay.
Rosy cheeks plunged into lovely hot towels
the evening is gone and it's time to pay.
Giueseppi always made such a fuss with free grappas and
                                                                 such
now it's so simple just pay and go
the table is wanted - we know, we know -
so
     Home James and don't spare the horses!
Tonight was our curry night.

THE OTHER HALF

     Men in conversation talk
of 'the other half.' Using her as an excuse
'Love to come but must ask the other half'
voice tailing off indicating forlorn hope
and thus passing the blame for non-attendance
when in very truth attending was simply unpalatable.
Or sometimes when on pleasure bent requesting the boon
                                                   companion
not to mention it to the other half
investing the adventure with a frisson of confidentiality.
Sub Rosa.
The title 'the other half' used for wife, live in
or regular companion.

     The other half
Held a different meaning to us in the city.
Lunch times spent in The Swan in Leadenhall Market
The Tyger on Tower Hill
or The Friars Crutch.
A triangle where a pie, cheese roll or smoked cod's roe
                                                   sandwich
was accompanied by half a pint of
Directors, Flowers Keggy Bit or 'Your Best landlord.'

The appearance of a colleague
meant putting aside the crossword and
partaking of 'the other half.'
A regular occurrence investing the drinking with
something more than just liquid to wash down
the food.
A custom, a man thing.

On Saturday's Old Uncle Fred
cap askew
would sit in The Cavalier
gazing into space
supping with relish first one
and then the second
Barley Wine.
until, glass empty
he would climb aboard his Mouton bicycle
pedal home
and cheeks flushed
take it out on
The Other Half.

THE DIVVIE

The boys call me Lovejoy and certainly I have the ability to
find the exceptional, the precious ones.
I do not confine myself to any particular classification or area.
Over the years I have discovered some exquisite oriental ones
Chinese, Malaysian even Japanese collectables and the very
best from Persia.
To say nothing of the finds from Florence Milan and Rome,
the iconic Russian
and the unforgettable from Vienna.
Let's not forget the West Indies too can yield treasure lest you
think my horizons are far flown let me hasten to say
I am equally at home with what this country has to offer.
Classic English Country style
that centuries of crafting have produced
from the Cotswolds and the Shire's
you see its not the place of origin that matters it's the treasure
each individual, never to be repeated.

Of course some flatter to deceive but I can quickly tell.
The pulse does not race
the spine tingling *frisson* is not there.
When it is, sometimes in the most unexpected places, _you
just know. Without seeing even, you know treasure's close and
you just have to look and listen.
Today I struck gold.
All the old feelings and then
at the back of shop in front of shelf marked literature
a slight movement.
Tall in a dress with heels enhancing the height
dark hair deep brown eyes long lashes and arched outlined
brows long strong fingers caressing a book
a slight quirk to the thin lips
said she was aware of my look.
No rehearsed patter or seeking to outrageously flatter just a
touch of sincerity and of course humour always works
for a divvie.
Euphoric that the gift is still there.
And then? I'd tell you after tonight's dinner But I never do.
Tell that is.

TRAVELLING

    A leisurely lunch then we window-shopped
and studied the Art Exhibition in the famous London Store,
critical she pronounced it crap.
In the jewellery section somehow her bag slipped to the floor
and burst open scattering the contents
kneeling to retrieve she parted company with her wrap.
The voice of the security man said 'Time for you to go.'
'I was just deciding to buy.'
He bent, handed her the plastic card that read
'Wanda's Party Dancers',
the nostrils sneered
'I don't think so, I think you had better leave.'
Treating her like a common whore.
She was never common.

    Later in the travel agents I stood by her as she ordered her flight.
'JKF, best available all the trimmings, the Big Apple waits.'
Knowing she was pot-less, seeing the strange name on the
credit card.
'What would you say', I asked, 'if I said make it two tickets.'
'It says a lot.'
The hand on my sleeve tightened
as the eyes filled with moisture
'I'll write, lift the telephone. . . . . and, promise
    . . . . .
    . . . . .
I'll be back'

THE NEWS TODAY

They've called the Last Post
for Barry the post.
His friends had missed him and were on the look
not knowing they had closed the book
on Barry the post.
What black despair brings a man to this.
No slash of the wrists or
pill over dose
only to be found, looked after and people
recognise a cry for help.
A gun is definitive.
I cannot say I knew him not rather
knew him a little found him pleasant
and now could say he didn't seem the type
any more than John who wired up the exhaust
or Stanley who took the final leap into the dark unknown.
May God save us from such a path.
We pray for
Barry the post
that he has joined the Heavenly Host
and found that peace that passeth understanding.

THE CHURCHES GREAT FOUNDATIONS

    The Churches great foundations
you serve them all your days.
You tight-knit band of helpers preserve the status quo.
Devoting your lives to the chosen furrow you must hoe.
You, May, do the flower rota
and watch with eagle-eye the arrival of the flowers
afterwards changing and arranging till they meet your exacting standards.
The hymn books also are in your remit and you guard them everyone
'gainst dog ears and grubby marks and strangers, counting them out
counting them back till the regular battle you have won -
it takes a lot of time but you give it gladly.

    As do you Charles regular and proficient organist.
Filling the church with Bach and Holy Passion until
the service starts and thin lips pursed in concentration
you play the appointed hymns daring the choir to keep up.
Two services every Sunday
and practice in between to say nothing
of weddings and funerals.
Much time is demanded of you and the organ.
You can scarce take a holiday.
Arthur knows how to repair the organ when it goes wrong
But is never allowed to play.
This Beethoven loving man lacks the presence, dresses
awkwardly and with his club-foot will not do.

As choirmaster Fred, every Tuesday you rehearse
the choir and more often than not seven 'till nine
stretches to ten and the altos pale
and exhausted toe your line.
Twice on Sunday your bass tones punch out the lines
In rhythmic but unmusical fashion.
At services end you talk with your choir and later
May and others in your chosen band.
Familiar faces in the congregation slip away
and your duties prevent you from speaking
with any newcomers.
Busy, busy, busy, who can take your place?

   The churches coffers are in your custody John
balancer of the books grudgingly you release funds
for heat and light making sure the boiler is not used before
mid October.
Church treasurer you squirrel funds away for vital fabric
repairs
check estimates closely and price the materials used.
A.G.M.'s committees, you sit on them all
enjoying the camaraderie of the little bank of helpers you hold
in thrall.

   Church secretary Phyllis you sit on all the committees
And take the minutes distribute notices, take instructions
From most in the cosy band of helpers you are in.
Even wearer of the cloth must watch his
Ps and Qs when facing your combined strength.

A band elect you jointly set the standards
That make for a comfortable church.
Keepers of the status quo - all else must go.
Newcomers who attend more than once warrant scrutiny
the less than savoury smelling somehow deterred
as are noisy and excitable young persons
and those who cannot sing in tune.
You are light hearted though despite all the work
making witty remarks about hideous hats
and garish coats.
Remember the woman who attended the W.I. in odd
and different coloured shoes?
And Bert in gale force wind
finding his bicycle veering across the road to deposit
him in the hedge.
How you laughed.
also - how could you forget -
The priceless occasion when Ernie, earnest Ernie
wanted a boys club he could grow into a Boys Brigade
Company
assembling his ragged collection of snotty nosed urchins
outside as the Girl Guides marched in.
How you laughed at his stupidity.
Later learning, with much hilarity,
how his simple wife managed to stick a safety pin
through a nappy and into the infants flesh!
Could not someone have helped her?
You may recall they drifted away and maybe found
or maybe not another church.

    The Churches great foundations
you serve them all your days.
Your loyalty not in question you take on every task
but never think to ask

    Why Jesus wept.

LAMPING

Jem holds the lamp and John the gun,
they shoot the foxes one by one.
Russet hued marauders who stalk like Assyrians
their quarry.
The indiscriminate slaughter in the hen house
the prolonged tussle with the hotel peacock
a young lamb or two
and of course, a rabbit.
Swiftly the indoctrinated cubs learn the habit
and the blood-letting grows
leaving in the morning evidence for the farmer and the crows.
Farmers bounty paid by the tail
a fresh pheasant skin creates a trail
led by the nose the foxes come to have their fun
transfixed in Jem's beam John kills them one by one.

IS THERE ANYBODY LEFT IN ALBANIA?

Is there anybody left in Albania?
Or Slovenia, Dalmatia and Estonia,
Lithuania, Moldavia, Romania and Transylvania
(excepting Vlad).
Like lemmings they gather at the frontiers of Uzbekistan
and have long been leaving old Iran.
In this modern gold-rush they seem quite mad.
They packed their bags and left Iraq
and safe over here laud their country to the sky's
but do not want to go back
- and there's a surprise.

Citizens of a mighty force
that, as Europe sees itself, on course
to be a major player on the world stage
with frontiers down they are free to roam
throughout Europe and call it home
the French and Germans seek to write new Europe's page
and so many others choose to pile
into this despis-ed little isle.
We native-born look warily at what Europe yields
confident we sup in Elysium fields
our laws are best our country pleasant and green
we know it's the best there's ever been.

'OLD KING COLE'

    Kenny Cole was rather big and also slow.
The teachers termed him backward
and blamed the bomb blast
and he sat in 4b with the other under-achievers.
The boys did not care, thought him fun to know,
and used him as the butt of many jokes.
On the way to school his cap would be snatched
from his head and flung from one tormentor to the next.
His legs, like his brain, did not work fast enough
and try as he might he never caught up or recaptured his cap
always having to pick it,
mud or chalk encrusted, from the gutter
when the teasers tired, discarded it and moved on.
The natural target for snowballs in winter his journey
to and from school must have been hell.
Sometimes hot with rage, barely coherent he would
utter dire threats.
Daily on the way they crossed the railway bridge
with the low brick parapet.
Mrs Reynolds was afraid he would throw a boy over
onto the line.
'Doesn't know his own strength, doesn't understand'.
The masters eyed a bigger frame than theirs and declined to
lend a hand.
'Mrs Reynolds understands 4b'.

    The years sped by and we moved on.
Kenny disappeared from sight and mind.
Looking back we too were afraid
to get too close
and I cannot think of one who was kind
To Kenny Cole.

Gossip said he became an electricians mate,
who married a beauty queen.
The years sped by and somehow he became
the biggest electrical contractor in the area.
When he bought the freehold the bank manager thought it great.
In rotary they called him King Cole.
He re-jigged the yard, called for 'his pipes'
and with ample stock at yesterday's prices
the plumbing division grew and grew
and Kenny became a merry soul
who enjoyed his fiddlers three.

The fiddlers three were:
Double invoice, Cash-in-hand and Quack Accountant.
The last a heavily built adenoidal myopic pebble lensed
bespectacled individual with flat feet
and great ability
to make figurers fly across the paper,
left to make things less and right to make things more.
Adroit at creating his extra supplementary bill he came
always late and never cheap.
But Kenny did not care.

Kenny did not care for he became a merry old soul
who, had just sold out for 3.4 million,
disposed of the villa in Spain, bought a house in Jersey
and looked forward to doing better than playing off nine.
His son had become a university don who
would never need the fiddlers three
which was fine, just fine
with Old King Cole.

DINNER FOR FIVE

Across the Cathedral Yard
this side of the guide and assembling party
I watched as people veered to left or right and drifted away
not wishing their morning to be marred
by anything uncomfortable.
As I stood motionless she moved directly towards me
holding hands with the child
whose pale face and expressionless blue eyes revealed nothing.
'Put a bit of heather in your shoes and it will help your back and knees.'
'Show me your palm - left one please.'

'You lost someone - this is your second marriage.'
Nodding towards my wife some way off
gazing in a shop window.
'She'll look after you and never leave you - she's good.'
'I know.'
'You're to stop worrying - you reap what you sow.
In two years time you have £28,000 coming
come here and give me £500.'
Addressing my just-arriving wife.
'How long have you been a Christian?'
No cross or bracelet on view.
'All my life.'
'You'll live to ninety-two.'
Back to me
'Give me some money for her dinner - I've five girls
- they need a dinner.'
'Are you a real Romany?'
' I am, I don't steal or do drugs.'
'Have you heard of Jacko Arnell?'
'My father's done up a wagon - varda.
All the painting, van, pots, milk churns, the lot.
What about the girls' dinner?'
Money covertly changed hands.
I could see where it was going, more than I can say for Oxfam.

    'Have you had any children?'
'No.'
'I see two girls, not little now.'
'Don't let them come knocking then.'

SHADES OF GILDAS

We were all handsome men.
All gentlemen then.
giving up our seats and rising when a lady entered the room.
Working hard and playing harder.
enjoying all that was in life's larder.
Appreciating art literature and music
perpetuating the life our fathers and older brothers fought for.
Hard to bare we will see it no more.
so where did we go wrong?

We tried with our children and their children - oh we tried
but the life and standards simple died.
An execution by cynical politicians
aided by greedy moneymen
who care not where they live as long as their coffers are full.
Country and honour sacrificed
and the young cannot write
but spend their time sending puerile texts
and communicate by making animal noises at one another
and know no law but grab.
But as we point the finger
do we ask who is really to blame?

Was our compass too small.
Could we have halted the erosion
by being more active on a bigger playing field.
The weak, the cowardly, maybe the wise
go lock stock and barrel and take up sojourn elsewhere.
France, Italy, Spain, of course Spain, or other foreign climes
and we few who treasure England stay,
But who hears our cries?

ON THE TRAIN

The little train was crowded to the gills.
They had swarmed out of the villages and the hills
Two coaches never would have been enough
Special offer guaranteed the journey would be rough.
£3.50 return from Barnstaple to Exeter was the lure
and it was pied piper time.

    An elderly lady had to stand all the way
whilst the young couple watched their children play
and sprawl over two seats and not learn the courtesy of
standing for a lady.
Almost a carriage length away we could hear
the four middle aged jolly boys shouting themselves
into the mood.

    At Exeter Central shoulders and feet
Devil takes the hindmost and they fell upon the city
like ravening wolves.
Coaches let loose the rugby supporters
Who pushed and shoved with the rest.
Every café pub and bar was full
with the pushing shouting, shouting, shouting horde
and the tills rang merrily.
At Michael Caines the restaurant was fully booked
with men and women ordering more and more
champagne and showing
the modern face of rugby.

Arms linked they walked three abreast
The pavement was theirs and to hell with the rest.
Hunters returning with the spoils -
signs to the station give direction
Bags from Jus 4 U, Girls are Us and Ugh - Connection.
The purchases made to satisfy their peers
no classics to defy the years
but just for the sake of a seasons fame.
Then 'its so you know - what a shame'.
Not even destined for the charity shops
but just dumped.

   Returning later the worse for wear
God made it rain hard - we didn't care.
The jolly boys trudged up the hill soaked to the skin
and we were safely gathered in.
Me? I recovered from a severe bout
  Of Ochlophobia.

A MAN OF THE TOWN

Perching on the barstool robust arms spread wide
holding up the broad sheet behind which he can hide.
He listens to the customers picking up the news
and gossip.
Trade ebbs and flows around him.
morning coffee's pastries, amuse bouche,
Kir Royal's, café cognac's
and omelette Arnold Bennett.
Morning through lunch, afternoon teas
and then the dinner menu.
he has created in this so historic town
an archetypal French café
and seen it flourish
as befits
A Man of the Town.

Satisfied things are working well
he prepares to promenade and with smile and
cheery word to those he knows
winds his way down the hill
to his delicatessen.
French bread flown daily from France
olives, pate's soucesse, and with a nod to tradition
and fashion, haggis.

    Cheeses from Europe jostle with English varieties
and tempt visitors and residents alike.
He checks the wines so carefully chosen
and the bottle conditioned ales.
Cosmopolitan tastes permit Punt e Mes, Noilly Prat
and Pineau Charentais
to stand companionably side by side whilst the sherry's
make room for the ports and Madeira's.
Comfortable with marketing and strategy now clearer
he resumes his tour -
    A Man of the Town.

A true boulevardier
But the gait points to Breton rugby of his youth
As does the hearty sense of humour.
No planning applications escape his notice
nor new business opening.
A prominent member of Rotary
Conscientious custodian of standards
a mover and shaker
he believes himself to be deservedly
    A Man of the Town.

COUNTRY LIVING

The morning sun shines on the glistening roofs and
waking buds
in Amberley.
Within curtain-drawn rooms weekenders stretch in bed
and contemplate the day.

Late Friday arriving they will rise by lunchtime
And the men will drink beer in front of the fire in the pub
And deny the regulars its warmth.
Meanwhile the women will prepare the food for the evening
they brought down from town
together with the wine.
Later joined by friends also from town
they will eat and drink merrily
and demonstrate their value to the community.

MOTHER'S DAY

Remember Mother's Day - show her how much you care.
Words in the window - guaranteed to make them stare.
Inside the cards were no good and the words were - Yuk.
Hannah found one with tasteful picture and by sheer luck
a blank inside.
Quickly she wrote
A Mother is a Girl's Best Friend
and signed it.
Matti found one similar and scribbled
A Mother is a Girl's Best Fiend.
Frowning she read it back
shook her head, decided it was appropriate,
licked and sealed the envelope.

SUMMER

Summer days, summer smells, summer remembrances.

High summer hot still air smells of parched garden
and brought to the surface foot scuffing chalk filling the
nostrils and slow days of boyhood mixture
of ennui and adventure.
Early dragging days of school holidays that
all too soon change pace
and gallop, towards next terms class changes and
unknown but feared lessons.
Boredom prompting catching the bus one short stop
to pour over the books
in the antique and second-hand tat, dank and dusty shop,
from where
adventure led, trotting the two miles to the park and
blowing hard
to spend sixpence hiring a rowing boat and playing
Swallows and Amazons
manoeuvring slowly across the sun-dappled arm-scorching
water,
lemonade bottle stowed beneath the legs.

Journeying to the summit of the North Downs walking in the
cooler lark-laden air
kings of the high ground not engaging in conversation but in
boyish fashion
inflicting monologues on each other all the time puffing on
dark bitter
Burma cheroots from the Co-op.

Running for the low-decker to wait for more and more passengers
each heavy footed causing the bus to lurch with their weight
rattling at last back to our own leafy roads.
In the evening tea replete allowed to hold the hose and filling the dry crevices
in the borders releasing the clove scents from the pinks and the moisture permeated
smells from the trees and grateful earth of summer.

Summer skies of cloudless blue and death bringing doodle-bugs.
Summer refuge sought with friends in rural Hertfordshire
the living room redolent of 'Uncle Bill's' fruity scented glass tobacco jar
whose owner rode the local range on the Liverpool Victoria bicycle.
Whilst we children roamed the heath burrowing in head topping bracken
crushing the fern fronds in warm hands to release the heady perfume.
Or perched in trees like nesting rooks
read our books
concealed by leaves and height
and smiled as beneath the tree
searchers called it was time for tea.

Summer teens, summer scenes and summer girls
In jodhpurs and gay dresses
some demure and some procasious
some flighty and sagacious.
River and down land excursions
learning to listen to another's list of wrongs and slights and verbal fights
triumphs and plans for the future and what might be
unfold over a tomato sandwich tea.
Ambition grows and creates an interest in clothes
intended to impress enabling us to belong, fit in,
play the game and seem
what we are not.

In Adult summers' the map is drawn the compass set
what has past is done but we need not forget.
Summer we can reason
is an annual recurring season
full of journeys, adventure, excursions
outdoor heart pumping exertions
sights, sounds, smells, smiles, slackness, sloth.

    Summer is Life.

CRISPIN SHEEPE
(Antique man of repute)

    Antique man of repute,
of this, he tells himself, there is no dispute.
Well known in the provinces
enjoying a certain cache with the London clique.
You would think by now he has it made
in this incestuous trade
and yet, and yet .....

    This long time practitioner has perfected the art
of a seeming lack of urgency
so that languor fits him like a glove
and serves him better than the push and shove
of competing lesser beings.
Careful to slip the w in cross
never appearing to be at a loss
the honed and modulated voice evolved from
close observation of the nobs
in the RAF with whom he did his national service
and the plump waist-coated bow-tied soft hand shaking
television appearing pundits who fill the screen
with unctuous bobs
demonstrating their expertise.
Invariably polite they treat him like their own
but never get too close and keep him on the fringe
he in turn heedful to reveal never a tinge
of jealousy or envy
acting as though in this select club
- but here's the rub -
of which he will never be a member.

The Georgian high street shop long gone
replaced by the riverside showroom with outside
staircase leading to the commodious flat above.
Comfortable in the long living room
reflecting back through the sped by years
the energy charged by money fears
heady days in Brighton
and the early time spent on the knocker.
The little house in Woodingdean
where he rejected all there was to be seen.

The anxious lady cried up 'there's nothing more'
as on a whim he slipped into the box room
to find behind the door
a Henry Fox.
Five pounds well spent
and now
from the wall by the dining area, its gazing cow
eyes him with content.

He has deliberated long over the Daks
or John G. Hardy, naturally tardy
as he watches through the window the like-minded
barely moving swan
and the sonorous tick of the long case reminds him
he should be gone.
A picture of studied elegance from the lemon
breast pocket hanky
to the slightly scuffed suede chukka boots
reaching for the seldom worn but oft displayed hat
that bears a hole but seems worth keeping.
Off to a meeting of his seeking.

Remembering back through the sped-by years
the marriage that ended in tears
but led to the long trail he had to follow
to acquire 'The Hare in the Hollow'
a painting not by Michael Jinks
but by the recently rediscovered April daughter
who calls herself Jarvis
and waits his coming.

    A glance at the quinquefarious walnut chest
and deep Peter Patching sofa
then hat in hand he heads for the train
picturing the renuent gesture sweeping the hair
from the cynical eyes as they meet again.
Hoping through art to be reconciled.
Father and his found again child.
Hoping in the years to come
when others may stay mute
she will in love on his cippus put
Crispin Sheepe
Antique man of repute

ANNIE PHOTOGRAPH

-1-

    Way back then
you were a stylish lady
in a becoming Bohemian way.
Your choice for work or play
the black knitted dress that complimented the
dark framed glasses
that tried to hide the humour in the brown eyes,
one of which had honeyed flecks.
Lethal pointed shoes with high stiletto heels
potential weapons on which you walked so easily
drawing the eye to the sheer stockinged classic legs
you called pins.
Mauve tinged lips
and matching finger tips
that drummed impatiently on my desk
or traced idle patterns in the ashtray
with a soon to be extinguished Rothman's kingsize.
Annie-office-worker-not yet twenty
for whom the world held plenty
of angst and frustration.

    The flat monochrome voice from Bow
not a sign of boredom indicating you wished to go
but your only way of expression
to turn the volume switch
up for punch-line or explanation
and for confiding or sombre moment
-     down just a titch.
You took me to the R.A. and the Tate

explaining Picasso's Blue Period
successfully concealing your own
beneath the ethnic beads and Chanel warmth
that charted your progress.
Hankering to be like your parents, Annie-the-Artist
but unable to paint a jot
chafing at the mundane jobs fate has cast instead as your lot.

-2-

    We saw Giant at the N.F.T.
-    free spirit you would ever be
in the evenings to party and show off your charms
in China town and Soho - up West with the best
then down East to jazz in the Watermens Arms.
Annie-good-time in the slit to the thighs Chinese dress.
Bridging the divide through Queenie Watts and Thelonius Monk
to Indian music and poetry with Mr R. Tagore
your life full of rhythm and culture galore
still unfulfilled with nothing to create.

    Your brother became a photographer
and used you briefly as a model
then you restless feet moved on and I saw you no more,
until today.
Annie-well-groomed-forty
assuredly lingering over a drink at Claridges.
Meeting eyes and a half smile were all we were able
to communicate
before you were called to your table.
Gucci bag, Versace dress, a very classy lady.
A model or designer? Did you make it on your own
find at last the outlet that led you on to fame?
Now for all the world to see
Annie-Photograph, you're in a silver frame.

TIME II

Tomorrow is when it will happen.
Tomorrow is when we achieve the achievable,
obtain the obtainable
sit at the pinnacle.
From earliest memory it has been tomorrow
that was promised.
The day of long trousers and pretty frocks,
bicycles and roller skates.
As the years passed by and we decided
it was still tomorrow.
The day we moved, or finally bought the dream car
the time for a career change, the time we made new friends.
The time lovers held open the door of possibility
saying 'Maybe tomorrow.'

Tomorrow may be the day we can
no longer run for a bus.
The day we give up tennis
prefer not to climb the hill.
So how do we deal with tomorrow?
By taking, it shaking it, making it
Today.

THREE BLIND MICE

    Quiet as mice they slipped over the border
from Wales into England.
Gliding through the thickets blending with the trees
careful to avoid the moonlight,
pausing as the other marauder glided overhead
listening to the owl hoot, waiting in case it concealed more
dangerous sounds.
They crossed at a point remote from castle and armed men
a full five miles from Chepstow.

    The Lord and his men had gone to Gloucester
on business of the King.
Left his wife to run the farm
with young strong Simon and aged Will
knowing she could come to no harm
for it was but five miles to Chepstow.

    Leaving the cattle they entered the yard
Simple Simon barred the way - 'Who's there?' he cried
and gurgled as he died
and the spear tore out this throat.
Old Will rushed - they tossed him in the midden
broke open the door
smiled and smiled at what they saw.
The lady in her night shift at the bottom of the stair.
One tore her shift in twain as she fled into the kitchen.
Without haste they followed
- she could not escape from there.
Eyed the big long table
planned to spread her wide and swythe her each in turn.
Slipping round the table
the wife seized the simmering pot
flung the contents in their faces
blinded and angry they fell upon her.
Hard and brisk was the strife
and the outcome bloody.
The farmer's wife cut off their tails with the carving knife.

    Emasculated all, they tried to crawl
across the border to safety and succour
three border raiders.

                  Three Blind Mice.

IRISH DANCING

They have fought for the bathroom
and are jostling for the mirror all the while
talking, cracking one liners raising a smile
the glue of competitive camaraderie moulding them close.
Lipsticks and gloss, hair sprays and perfumes
Je Revien, Charlie and Organza
each head lining the wearer's personality.
They all went to Friday late-nights at Chico's
and had their hair done by the best stylist in town. . .
. . .Angela on again about going to university in England
to read architecture or law
- at any rate to enter a profession.
She's talking big but no matter,
they've known her since her first confession.
Dressed to the nines, especially Kiera who
persuaded cousin Helene to break the chain
of wedding dress orders and do a special creation in gold and black.
A few more minutes and they will be ready, with a mirror-wards last glance
to sally forth - going to The Dance.

    Pink cloakroom tickets on arriving
and a queue for the ladies
at last entering the hall with languorous but wary cat like gait
cool. cool.
absorbing the music and the people. . . .
warm-up band Little Billy Bigallo and his Boys
- he's bound to play some hip-hop
- sometimes plays too loud
cool, cool,
three sassy girls in the crowd.

    A sudden flurry as more people enter,
Meg accompanied as usual by Uncle John,
they have been courting for years,
her father was against it but now he's gone
they don't seem to be in any hurry.
Going with the flow, swaying to and fro
carving out some space, being in the know
what's coming next from Billy Bigallo.

    They have danced with one another
then with Patrick's brother
now it's getting crowded and they are being taken up
as main band Cats Whiskers gets into its stride
so many people it's easy to hide
from the ones you don't fancy.

    Stamping and whomping - and expert footwork
from the blond Hennessy brothers who (rightly) think it a
perk to dance them off their feet - and then what a treat
enfolded close to the gold medallion, sharp cut black trews
half hearing the chatter, well rehearsed patter
as he seeks to beguile
bending down and smiling that dark gypsy smile
as all the while;

the multicoloured spinning light reaches out,
the orb, all conquering twinkling ball
pulls and plucks her
right out of his arms, out of the hall
and right out of the world
into the stratosphere
above the pink clouds and marshmallow castles. . . .
three sparkling girls
hot, hot, hot.

   The evening is passing in a whirl
the hours are running as they twirl
it seems every man in town is here tonight.
Partners galore all on the floor.
A floor full of fellers
with a lot of late entries
and a strong smell of drink,
so flookered they can hardly stand.
it's last waltz time proclaims the band
joined in the finale by Billy Bigallo's Boys.
Earlier she'd left him hung out to dry
thinking, maybe I'll get to him bye and bye
- and now's the time!

   Joined at the cloaks by Maeve and redhead Terry
lights dimming as the noisy crowd spills out with men
lurching and making their play.
Suddenly the girls are off like rockets
remembering the Mammy's warning -
'Beware of men with sticks in their pockets!'

TIME III

'The little hand's on Mickey Mouse and
the big hand's on Donald Duck.'
Gradually the child learned the twelve-hour clock.
Enjoyed stumping through the rustling multi-coloured leaves that
filled the gutters and the grass verges on the way to school.
Later becoming familiar with the twenty-four clock
and discovered how to set time by the sun and shadow.
Encountered the joys of sport, running and cycling,
all the time aware of the birds in the skies above.
Their mating, hatching and migration when armies would
sit on telephone wires and wait the signal to depart.
Their space occupied by Brent geese who arrived on cue
seeking a warmer clime.

    The landmark occasion slipped by unsought, unmarked, unnoticed
as intended.
Afterwards life was just the same
the pleasures still there, the contents of the glass tasted
just as sweet.
Some things had had their day and were good recollections.
Spring and youth went together.
Summer typified the high roller times
when all was possible, achievable and available,
the days long and full.

    Autumn stealthed in like the piano
replicating the tenor sax note
the change like the seasons barely noticeable.
The hedgerows and the harvests bountiful
the granaries of the mind full.
Sweet the air, clear the skies
the urge to start another enterprise.
The energy for yet another adventure.
Life is the same,
the unchanging trees high on the sky-reaching downs
watered by a little lad
planted in a ring.
One more unchanging pleasurable thing.
in this most colourful time.
Life is sweet
and winter is a long way off.

WISE MONKEY

Me ah see nothing.

Jimmy walking towards me fast like skipping
I get ready with the with the wit
when suddenly he cross the road
Jimmy and Mr Come and Go giving the high fives.
How come he even know such company.
Then - I see how he's dressed
                    in the money.
Sharp jacket, watch, rings, neck chain
all over bling bling.
While they parleying I slip by unnoticed
go home to ponder.

Tuesday night Crab and Lobster Restaurant burn down.
I stand in the crowd next morning.
Watching the smoke eddy from the caved in roof
of the flat above.
Hearing Dopy Desmond say the owner, Guy
for some time bin playing away.
Seeing Mr Come and Go hands in overcoat pockets
and Jimmy acting like they don't know one another.
Not acquainted.
Tomorrow I move to Sussex.
New Job new home
lots of country and sea air.

Me - ah see nothing.

MY HOUSE

My house nestles in the High Weald.
Mellow red brick drowsing in the afternoon sun.
The open windows allow the spice and nutmeg smells
from the pinks to fill the room with fragrance
as I discard the paper and begin a journey
re-visiting all the mind will yield.

Travelling through the one street villages with
special friendly shops.
Passing the hammer-ponds, climbing to high
Ashdown Forest ridge walking the hundred acre
and throwing Pooh sticks from the bridge gazing
at the fields where once we camped remembering the
route from now closed station we once tramped.
Through pretty Mayfield to Batemans there to follow
the ancients trail from Pooks Hill down to Storrington
below the cloud capped Downs.

My house lies in the lee of the sheltering South Downs
and is so shaped that it has what aunts once termed
a morning room. The front faces the Downs and in early
summer it is comforting to smell the log smouldering
in the grate the smoke informing all that I am home.
From the galleried landing I see not the towns
but the ascending trails and watch Ben walking his dog
or the cyclist selecting a low gear
pedalling rhythmically until the top is near.

To walk along the grass and chalky way looking down
on all is to feel near heaven, the wind on the face
lark singing cloud scudding care flying free striding
heaven knowing that destination is not heavens gate
but drink and vittles providing Eastbourne.
Knowing that this reluctant traveller travels
the way to home. The home he has yet to find
constantly journeying in the mind
unable to decide but always accompanied by hope.

THE MAN FROM HEATHFIELD

    With fatigued squeals it pulled into the station
as though in pain.
Neatly folding The Times, leaving it on the seat
he unhurriedly stepped off the train,
watching the small clutch of passengers filter through the exit
making his leisurely way past the door marked 'Gentlemen'.
Emerging later to proceed unnoticed through the station
approach
onto the road
towards his destination.

    A five and a half-hour journey
for the trouble-shooter who long ago made the decision
never to work his own patch.
The contacts and the contracts always come to him
he waited for their plans to hatch
then the contacts and the contracts came to him,
who stated he was never cheap, but always good
- success made his reputation -
and now on leaving the station -
The man from Heathfield was on his way
going to earn his pay.

Mr Brandon was a man of substance, well thought of in the town
he had built a sizeable business and was prominent in Rotary
charitable and gregarious with fingers in many pies.
The club red leather armchair
comfortably accommodated his increasing size
and was positioned so that he might
admire the well tended garden and see the mantelpiece
French clock well content with his state.
A man of habit he heatly folded The Times, placed it on the table
and substituted the Church's slippers for well polished brogues,
donned, the well cut sports coat with gold watch and chain
secured in the lapel,
then the Aquascutum topcoat,
said good-bye to his wife
and left in ample time not to be late
for the forthcoming appointment.

   Saturday evening was his regular 'time off'
allocated to a convivial glass or two with friends,
ears attuned to pick up on any new commercial trends
or a business deal to broke.
Early evening was best before the space became crowded
and the establishment noisy.
Proceeding up Bread Street relishing 'his time'
pausing briefly by the off licence window
before the last little climb
into the High Street
where as always he admired the view of the church clock.

The man from Heathfield
relished the hint of frost found in the misty gloaming,
sauntered from Cross Street into the High Street,
pausing briefly to take in the chemist's Tudor front
and admire the view of the church clock.

Brandon crossed the road by the post office
and stepped beneath the arch that led to the car park
and lounge bar entrance of the old coaching inn,
The Crossed Keys.
Half turning in response to the civil
'Mr Brandon a moment please'
then, *he shot him in the head*
with his experience not needing to check he was dead,
and with unhurried gait
he strolled down Challis Lane
knowing he would not be back again
pacing the three miles to the out of town bus stop from where
circuitously
he could travel to a different railway station
and with luck not be too late
arriving at his destination.
The man from Heathfield was going home.

IN THE CLUB

'I've joined the Club' he said waving his yellow book
preparing to stop on the corner
where the keen wind flattened his trousers revealing the
sparrow thin legs within.

The book was an unusual shade
not the yellow of buttercups or daffodils
not lunar cool Lover's moon Hunter's moon Bomber's moon
not of the low in the sky November lingering into December
angry sun ambushing motorist with blinding burst below
the ineffectual sun visors or
flickering through the trees with epilepsy inducing rhythm.
Not the canary hue of smart waist coats
sported by gentlemen in well cut tweeds
and not the
shade of comfortable knotted pullovers worn beneath the jackets and blazers by
Jolly old boys laughing and wheezing filling the lounge bar
of the Steam Packet assuaging their throats with
gin and tonics and single malts.

The colour was like none of these,
garish, right in the face, intended to be noticed,
the passport to entry to
the anti-coagulant clinic,
to be carried at all times
a record of medication that will go on and on
forever and anon.

QUONDAM TRAVEL

    Tread softly for you tread on my dreams,
when you invaded I was travelling
and again with the girls I knew
the vivacious energetic girls, ready smiling laughing dancing tripping
all day long girls
and the music loving classic loving jazz loving bohemian swaggering girls.
Blue-eyed blond haired conquerors and dark curled brown-eyed sorcerers
filling the days with laughter and the nights with love.
The girls who wore Je Reviens, Chantilly, L'Air du Temp and of course Givenchy
like skins you could sink into and become engulfed in fragrance.
Still the same age as then they have not changed but I
I, less gauche more knowledgeable, sympathetic, mature, confident.
    Tread softly as you leave and I resume my journey.

TUBBY TAYLOR

Tubby Taylor is what his class mates called him
and Tubby Taylor became his name
to all the school the same.
In truth not so much fat as burly
with a frame that in adulthood would make him a natural
                                                          heavyweight.
On the periphery of our younger vision
two or three years older he had no part in our lives
living nowhere near I know not what caused the decision
to walk down Boundary Road

Saying goodbye to a friend I said within earshot
'that's Tubby Taylor.'
Pausing for me to reach him, once cornered
he then launched into a savage attack
punching me about the head face and body
pushed me violently into the hedge
and strolled on.
Heart pounding, trembling, bruised and close to tears
trying to quench my boyhood fears
I watched him pass our home
which seemed like another insult.

Shortly after he left school
passing from my life but not my ken.
The humiliation, unspoken of humiliation left a scar
and in the memory bank revisited from afar.
I did not pursue him down the years and labyrinth ways
but like any hound sought the scent
knowing that when we next met and the quarry caught
I would be the aggressor, launching the assault
with forearm smash or straight fist breaking the nose
inflicting damage - life had taught me how when I chose.

Then last week I found him.
My resolution was steel and I manoeuvred into position
eye contact said he did not recognise me
and I would have to explain after the attack.
Balancing nicely I stepped forward. . . .

Afterwards I could not believe I had simply
turned on my heel and walked away.
I could have gone though with it I swear
can only think that possibly, possibly,
what put me off

was the wheel chair

SUSSEX PAEN

Oh to be in England now that April's there
but oh to be in Sussex and smell the South Downs air
to watch the larks ascending and listen to their song
followed by the hang gliders who soar 'bove Steyning Bowl
to tramp the South Downs Way from morn till evensong.
Harting Down to Bury Hill and then descend
climbing by High Titten and then to wend
our way.
Kithurst Hill revealing Parham deer below
Chancton Bury Ring, Pyecombe, Lewis, the miles roll by
from Alfriston only a few more to go.
Into the Sun down Beachy Head
to Eastbourne for food and rest.
The South Downs, the South Downs Way is best.

What of the Weald?
you hear men cry.
Oh yes we wot of the Weald.
Through Burwash Weald to Kipling land at Batemans.
Look for the ancients on Pooks Hill
then Danehill to Chelwood Gate and glorious Ashdown Forest
Pooh Bridge and five hundred acre wood.
My friend, you and I could
be like Belloc's Four Men and philosophize.
Step with me if you please.

    From the Gallipot to the Haywaggon
and the Anchor in Hartfield
to Withyham's Dorset Arms
you will quickly recognise
good pubs, good Sussex pubs are these
In which to sup and take our ease.

    Then in winters dark sheltered in the Downs lee
Storrington Steyning Fulking and Poynings
make snug homes for folk like you and me.
Wood smoke, lights, bells - as Christmas hangs in the icy misty air

Give praise for Sussex and being there.

ST VALENTINE'S DAY

    Mainly mature couples decorously dining
not now for unrequited love still pining
or clubbing and dancing feverishly to the unrelenting beat
twirling in the dark and ever increasing heat.

    No, these are comfortable celebrants
enjoying the good things of life
relaxing in the bar with drinks and nibbles
studying the menus and scanning knowledgably the wine list.
Shown to their tables where every lady is presented
with a rose.
An evening of good food and drink and warmth.

    Amongst the sprinkling of younger couples
one pair stand out.
Voluptuous in a clinging low cut red dress
the mammalian orbs seemingly swell with passion
and the attentive clean cut swain blessed with good fortune
enjoys her laughter, smiles and gaiety.
Between courses crossed legs
enabled her to swing an elegant high heeled
red shoe that matches her dress.
Somehow transcending the subdued lighting
her sparkling brown eyes and white toothed smile
light up the room.
As meals end he disappears and returns
announcing his presence
with the lightest of touches
as he hands her, her crutches.

OLD ERNIE

He lived across the road
in an identical house to ours.
A long-term resident known to my folks as a good neighbour
Ernie Pearson.
Then came the day
when I knew him too but in a different way.

   Back from National Service
re-acquainted with the rows of terraced houses
the plane trees and neatly clipped green or gold privet hedges
that fronted and flanked the small gardens
I became a commuter, a worker in the city.
The platform meeting
at Streatham Common Station prompted the greeting
'Good morning Mr Pearson', 'Good morning young man'.

   Swiftly it became a shared journey
in an eye smarting smoke wreathed compartment
we glanced at our newspapers,
raised voices and talked together
and with a good hearted tweed suited yellow fanged
roll your own chartered surveyor
and rattled our way to London Bridge.
A daily ritual broken once by me
when from the arriving before ours Victoria train
a dark curled head was thrust
and my name called
running up the platform leaping through the open door
squeezing next to Avril chatting as before
yet too inhibited by the other passengers stares
to renew an old relationship.
I just arrived late at the office.
My abrupt leaving enhanced my reputation
the morning greetings were warmer
and I was enrolled as a helper.

Ernie had an operation for something down below
debilitated he needed support
embarrassed, I barely acknowledged the pointed hello
of swifter passing colleagues
and we arm in arm slowly paced our way over London Bridge
staying linked through Leadenhall Market
where he bought his cigarettes.
20 Lambert and Butler straight cut
and on Fridays double packs
released at last as we entered St Mary Axe.
Into his office then into Lloyds
where he was not a name but definitely a face
a man of influence

   Sometimes on the long march
we would fall in with Ernie's friend
The well cut suit grey overcoat and shining grey hair
Went with the contented confident ambassadorial air
A sleek city cat.
Both it seemed were local councillors
Disturbed to hear of my attempts to buy a house,
Applying for a Local Authority mortgage
only to be thwarted by the estate agent
Who pushed his building society
and explained that he could guarantee
The Local Authority scheme was not for me
Friends on the inside, a man of influence.
It could not be, they shook their heads, that such a louse
Could influence a decision.
The Authority was above reproach, they treated with derision
The agents claim, 'a word with John would just confirm'.
My loan came through
and we moved in just as the agent's office closed.
He and I had brushed with men of influence.

    At Election time we delivered leaflets,
helped in the local office
and accompanied Ernie and his wife to the count.
Then to the Stork Club
to celebrate with smoked haddock and poached eggs.
Seeing the good times roll.
At home relaxed in lambs wool grey cardigan
In repose he sometimes assumed the look of a friendly sheep
then the blue eyes would twinkle
and he again became Old Ernie.
The years rolled by and the Party and the Council and the
City took their toll.
The years rolled by and he and I both moved
both hoping to see again the good times roll.

    Ernie retired to Worthing,
watched the sea from his comfortable flat.
Relaxed in the autumn sunshine
accompanied Maisie to Marks and Spencer
entertained the visitors from London, enjoyed the chat.
Went on little excursions but was now quite short of breath.
Came the day he collapsed on getting out of bed
the doctor came, shook his head
and pronounced Old Ernie dead.
To go like that was a tragedy simply not his way.

He sat bolt upright on the mortician's slab.
After some debate he persuaded them to get Maisie and a cab.
Old Ernie then went home to die another day.

TELL ME ABOUT JO'BURG

'So you're from Cape Town?'

'Witwatersrand.'

'Whatever.'

'But I spent a lot of time in Jo'burg. Great place to live
I had my own flat, good job, great social life!
Parties all the time!
You would have loved it.'

'I give fantastic parties - you must come to my next one -
maybe next week. Hey! I knew a South African woman once,
she had this record,
song, about this boy who is looking forward to being taken
into town
and he's going to have ice cream, pop and bubble gum. You
must know it, it was
a big hit.'

'In my mother's time! Woman? She was probably as old as
my mother.'

'Ask your mother to my party.'

'You're sick!'

'Lots of people be there, cricketers lawyers, actors, all sorts. I'm inviting Lois, you know, tall girl - librarian.'

She's a horse!'

'Horse's gallop.'

'You're sick!'

'We've got this pond in the conservatory, I'll drain it, fill it with champagne - we'll have an orgy!'

'You're definitely sick!'

'What are you doing?'

'Don't you want a tidy bed? Man with your social standing?'

'You look great in that uniform.'

'Here we go! Show a man a uniform and he turns into a lecher! You *can't* help it - all men are sick!'

'If you don't want to be looked at why do you pull the belt so tight?'

'Because my waist is so tiny!
Listen darling I must go.'

'When am I going to get out of this place?'

'Ask Dr Morgan.
I really must go darling. See you tomorrow.'

. . . .

'Tell me about Jo'burg.'

THE RELICT

It's been two long years and the way is still not clear.
Two new calendars hung since that fateful year.
More used now to staying in
but not entirely comfortable
-    heaven knows she's tried to build a life.
(If nature abhors a vacuum why does it not fill this void?)

At first here was so much to do
and she was busy all the time.
Dealing with the paperwork
listening intently to the grave professional advice
that went in one ear and out the other.
Subconsciously wishing he could still take it all away,
make it all seem simple, and with a smile
create a bright new day.
The kind friends who 'just popped in to see she was alright'.
The invitations to lunch or dinner
contrasted with those who found if difficult
to place a lone female at their table.
(Did they regard her as competition - preposterous
were they not friends!)
Distancing herself as soon as she was able
from them and the surprising men
who called to give sympathy or help
overstaying, steering the conversation
and making it plain they had a yen
to make her the girl they went home from.

Some people she noticed, crossed the road
and affected not to see
but she understood
their empty minds and embarrassment
at being close to the real world.

    She still attended church
but the message seemed at a tangent.
Was jollied into the lunches
and meetings of the Towns Women's Guild.
Tried her hand at quilting
but the company had her wilting
marvelling at their expertise and dedication.
Last summer she chummed up
with a member of the Guild
and the pair shared a cabin and cruised the Med
on the Sunbird.
A surfeit of food and sun
then her plenteous wardrobe and best frocks
enabled her to shine in red
and grace his table when seated next to the captain
at dinner.
The excursions to historic places and shopping trips were fun
But eventually the interlude was done,
finished.
Save for the Christmas card from John and Jacqui,
cruise mates from Northampton.

    This year she is resolved to get fit
and join the Ramblers
so she's walking everywhere.
Yesterday crossing the churchyard to the High Street
with a list of what she wanted there
she read not for the first time
but for the first time comprehending.
The tombstone of the Leigh's

> John Henry 1822-1884. Beloved husband.
> Charlotte Agnes, Relict 1826-1897
> Called to Heaven.

Feeling uplifted, strangely comforted - striding out boldly.
Thinking, that's what I am, two years widowed
        Relict of this Parish

BREAKING BREAD

    Breaking bread my love is harder
than breaking hearts.
Why should I be so stubborn
when just for a few hours
I can be pleasant and charming
just for you.
They are not so bad, they are your friends
who I have met before, so why the fuss.
    Why break your heart.

    There is no fuss.
Don't you think I have played
this game before.
Many, many times over.
Don't you know I have a history
of dissemblement.
Don't you know sooner or later
I have ceased to play the game
and become true to myself.
Don't you know it is not conscience
or moral rectitude that prevents me
playing a part for one brief hour.
Don't you know it is me being me.

Don't you know I care for you
but not enough you say
for this eccentric Englishman to
don a mask, play a part, be what I am not.
Perhaps, meeting them in the street
or at the theatre bar
encountering them in the company
of other friends from afar.
Don't you know the sacred rule.
Do not break bread
with those who are not friends.
Do not break bread
with a dishonest fool.

A BAWD'S EYE VIEW

She's seventy two and proud of it
and not too old for a bout of it
if she can find a man who is up for it
strong and hungry enough to cope with it
and she's always on the look.

    The window cleaner will run a mile
as fast as you can blink and smile
with relief that he has survived the trial
done the front and the back - taken his small pile
of hard earned loot
- and gone.

It's not Amsterdam
but she gives not a damn
for yesterday.
Sits in the window the better to see
in the passers by a likely he.
The clock strikes half three
it's time for tea
and all she can see
are the big college lads larking and shouting with glee
on their way home.

When she moved in the carpenter came
but it wasn't the same
as in Cheam where she built her fame.
He produced his notebook and talked of V.A.T.
- didn't seem to know what he was at.
Couldn't catch up with the conversational game,
did the wardrobe - but his excuses were lame
and he won't be back again.

    Tomorrow's Friday and she won't be alone
but 'Entertaining Mr Sloane'.
    Tomorrow's Friday and the Insurance Man
- who doesn't look like an also ran -
is coming to review her affairs
- and they both had a laugh when he put it like that
it will be at half-eight,
she will bet he won't be late
and will offer a single malt or ask if he will join her
in a large G and T.
He is certainly not a cup-of-tea.
He is leery and will try and sell her a bond,
it will take more than one visit and they could
get quite fond
of entertaining one another.
Well, what she is plotting is not a crime
and which ever way it goes it will be

        Premium Time.

DEVONSHIRE DUMPLING

Boy's don't start to panic, don't take fright
The Devonshire Dumpling's out tonight.
She may look plump she may look round
but her legs are strong and her wind is sound.
She'll keep on dancing through the night
of pleasure she'll take a healthy bite
when others flag and need a rest
she's still twirling with the best.
Taking her drink like any man
feel sorry for those that turned and ran
flashing teeth and smile set the room aglow
she's fun to be with, fun to know.
You wanted a bit of life and you got a bit of life
Just think of the man that gets her for a wife.

KNOCK, KNOCK - WHO'S THERE?

Monday through to Friday were days of daily toil
Saturday was for the garden and generally pottering around.
Sunday he regarded as his day, early morning cycle ride
luxurious bath and cooked breakfast then
armchair deep and feet up with *The Sunday Times*.
The knock presaged in-law visitors
and Sundays started to spoil.
They came at eleven and were still going strong
at half past three
coffee and snacks, and they were still there for tea!
departing taking with them most of his Sunday
leaving *The Times* consumed in small doses right up to
Thursday;
he remained affable.

The new neighbours across the road were friendly
and on Saturday came the knock
'Look it's Jim.' 'Just called for a natter,
unless you're busy?' 'No it really doesn't matter.'
Strolling in the garden talking rubbish.
one man's priorities are another man's oblivion.

Knock, knock on a week-day evening around half past eight
produced Jim's wife who immediately enmeshed them
in her world of recalcitrant kids, irritating husband
slow buses and stupid people in the estate agents where she
worked
part time
and a whole list of other things to hate.
Opening the front door when she did at last depart
he remained affable.

Knock, knock and one evening visit became three out of five
smelling of garlic and afternoon whisky
with her jarring Antipodian accent it was talk, talk
- and the pub too far for a walk -
eventually departing with the quip, 'I may be over tomorrow
maybe to borrow
the proverbial cup of sugar.'
Somehow he remained affable.

   Fog disrupted the train service
standing in the milling crowd watching the departure board
she suddenly appeared at his side.
With half an hour to wait he took her off for a drink.
On the train she naturally talked incessantly
travel rattle drowning her words but giving him time to think
ignoring her heavy breasted forward slouch and crooked grin
he nodded where he thought appropriate.

   The following day working from home
he formulated his plans.
Resolved to stop the visits even if it ended in sorrow
he would put it to her she could no longer borrow
the proverbial cup of sugar.
Seeing her return from the estate agents in the early afternoon
waiting ten minutes for her to settle
then, no longer affable
he crossed the road
opening the door to his knock she said
'I was beginning to think you would never come.'
turning to lead the way upstairs.

CHARLIE

Charlie is my darling, my darling, my darling
and every day
in every way
I love him more and more.
His treacle toffee eyes
seem to follow me about
and when we are apart
he wrenches at my heart
and I think of my fingers in his silken hair

The old biddy down the lane
says we are walking out,
he never even glances but keeps his head up high
and we both ignore her arch ness.
Charlie comes from a very good family
and I am so lucky he chose me.

Oh Charlie is my darling
- I will be his wag
and no doubt get a return
from my very special darling
for Charlie is my darling
    my bold Cavalier.

FOLLOW THE STAR

-I-

In the beginning there was the star
shining to the north
illuminating the way to a city
in a foreign clime.
The advent of the trains shrank the journey
to an acceptable time.
Once I travelled on the express train
from London to Edinburgh
being already familiar with part of the line.

In dark days I sought refuge with friends
in Oaklands, in Hertfordshire
near Old Weywyn village outside the Garden City.
Greenlines ran to Oaklands
and the single-decker green bus was warm,
somewhat exclusive
from Victoria Coach Station
hurrying through London, suburbia and country before
stopping outside the grocers
who sold cakes and paraffin each smelling of the other.
Near by the pub
an entrancing child denied establishment
called the North Star.
The footpath by the side and a mile walk led
to home and safety.

Weekend visits and a faster journey proved
the train was best
hissing, puffing, smut scattering, rhythmically speeding
through dark innumerable tunnels
arriving at length at Welwyn North Station
and a waiting friend
a down hill walk
through woods and the lane, Turpin's Ride, to arrive again
at the North Star

-II-

Later a three month sojourn, called private evacuation
in which we roamed
free as birds over Potters Heath
and an area from Codicote to Welwyn,
climbed trees, built camps
safe from the threats from VIs and experienced
country peace, country heaven,
and enjoyed the fruits of the initiative driven 'brown market.'

    Last year a return visit was made by car.
Past friends all scattered
mature trees cloak the heath in shade,
more houses, detached all,
somnolently bake in the afternoon sun
behind remote controlled gates
more shops and a revised enlarged flower vista'd
welcoming North Star pub
with a sign depicting a steam locomotive
call the North Star.
Was there such a train that once plied the long journey to
Auld Reekie?
An anorak will inform.
Vastly changed Oaklands that somehow, somehow,
hold its old magic

FINE FARE

I need to be watered and fed
smoked salmon - champagne to go to my head
Treat me right and I could stay all night
as we progress from fed to bed.

Lazarus Press